visiting
SICILY

ARNONE Editore - Palermo

© Copyright 1999 by ARNONE Editore s.r.l.
Offices and Administration: Via Francesco Crispi 120 - 90139 Palermo (Italy) - Tel./Fax 0916 124 007
Depot: Via Filippo Patti 25 - 90133 Palermo - Tel. 091 333 461 - Fax 091 333 484
www.arnoneeditore.com • Email: info@arnoneeditore.com

Texts: Mario Kos - Lanfranco Angeli
Translation: Quid, Traduzioni e Servizi Linguistici - Palermo (C. Ricchiari)
Graphics and cover: Saverio Rao

Photolithography: Litoscanner, Palermo
Printed by: Officine Grafiche Riunite - Palermo

Photographs by Lanfranco Angeli
Aerial photographs: Aut. SMA No. 1226 of 17-12-1991.

*Photographs on pp. 17 top right and left, 21, 22 top, 23, 24 top, 26 top, 27 bottom, 28 top, 29, 38 top,
39 top, 52 top, 53, 65, 89, 101 top left, 135, 144 top, 206/207 by* Paolo Arnone.
Photographs on pp. 16 bottom, 22 bottom right, 36 top, 36 bottom left, 79 by Carmelo Sammarco.
Photograph on pp. 59/60/61 by Enzo Lo Verso.
Photographs on pp. 72, 73, 77 bottom, 81 top, 83 by Foto Sansone.
*Photographs on pp. 3, 4, 13, 24 top and bottom right, 51 top and bottom left, 85, 123 bottom,
140 right, 152 left, 154 middle left, 154 right, 155 top, 156, 183 by* Foto Patti.

All photographs property of ARNONE Editore.

ISBN 88-87663-08-4

Sicily

GEOGRAPHY - HISTORY - ART - TRADITIONS

Syracuse Archaeological Museum: Polychrome terracotta frieze with the Gorgon, sacred area of the temple of Athena.

Geography. Sicily (formerly Sicania and Trinacria) is the largest (25,460 sq km) and most important island in the Mediterranean, where it occupies a central position. Around it are a number of archipelagos which administratively belong to the island: the Lípari or Aeolian islands, Ustica, the Égadi and Pantellería, and the Pelagie. Sicily is a region of volcanoes. The highest is Etna (3,370 m), a solitary relief near Catania. Other volcanoes have formed some of the minor islands: all the Lípari islands, Ustica, Pantellería. Some of these are still active (Strómboli and Vulcano) or dormant, while others have been extinct since time immemorial. In addition to Etna's imposing volcanic cone, Sicily has four mountain groups. The first (the Sicilian Appennines) stretches along the north coast, from the Strait of Messina to the Torto River, as a continuation of the Calabrian Appennines. It is divided into three sections: the Peloritani, the Nébrodi (or Caronie) and the Madonie, and its highest peaks rise to about 2,000 m. The second group encircles the western part of Sicily, to the west of the Torto and Plátani rivers. The third mountain group forms the heart of the island, and overlooks the African Sea to the south-west; its most characteristic part is often referred to as the "sulphur-bearing upland". The south-east corner of Sicily is mostly characterized by a plateau (Hyblaean Mountains). The island has little flat land. The largest stretch, 430 sq km, is the Catania Plain, lying between Etna and the mountains of the province of Syracuse. Other flat areas lie in the province of Trapani, near Marsala, Mazara and Castelvetrano, whose fertile red soil nurtures the world-famous grapevines. Similar features are found in the areas surrounding Scoglitti and Vittoria, in southern Sicily. The major rivers are the Salso (or South Imera) and the Plátani, but they are almost dry in summer. The climate is typically Mediterranean along the coasts, with hot but not torrid summers, mild and short winters, and moderate rainfall (from October to March). The annual average of clear days is 98 in Palermo; 110 in Messina; 130 in Taormina; 133 in Syracuse. The annual average temperature along the coasts is between 17°C and 18.7°C, July being the hottest month. The typical evergreen Mediterranean scrub vegetation is widespread. There are still traces of the oak-woods which must have covered the lower mountains in ancient times, as well as of the beech-woods which form the upper belt of the Nébrodi and Madonie woods. Among the cultivated species is the ash, flourishing on the slopes of the north coast. The olive-tree and the vine were introduced in ancient times (from the Near East), as were the almond-tree, the pistachio, the pomegranate and the hazel (imported from Campania). Other species imported from the East include the carob, the sumac, the palm-tree (though its fruit rarely ripens), the mulberry, the lemon tree and the bitter orange. The sweet orange (Portogallo) was brought from China by the Portuguese only in the 16C, while the tangerine was imported from Madura (Sonda) about two centuries ago. The holm oak is especially widespread at altitudes between 300 m and 600 m. Cork-woods are also present.

History. The first inhabitants of Sicily were the Sicans, Elymi, Ausonians and Sicels. But it was only with the arrival of the Greek colonizers that Sicily entered "Great History" (8C BC). The Greeks founded almost all the first Sicilian cities along the coast: Naxos, Syracuse, Lentini, Catania, Messina. Their inhabitants, in turn, founded new cities: Taormina, Megara Hyblaea, Gela, Selinunte, Himera, Milazzo, Agrigento, Segesta, Lilybaeum, etc. These cities were first ruled by Oligarchies and later by Tyrannies. The most powerful Tyranny was that of Syracuse, which eventually subjugated all the other cities. But it soon came into conflict with Carthage, which had managed to consolidate its presence in the western tip of Sicily, taking control of Motya, Panormos and Solunto. The conflict ended with the victory of the Syracusans in the battle fought at Himera (480 BC). The war between the two powers, however, continued with alternating fortunes until Rome took the place of Syracuse, inheriting its historical role. Only after the three Punic Wars and the destruction of the Carthaginian Empire did the Romans gain effective control of Sicily. The

*Palermo Archaeological Museum: Metope with
Zeus and Hera on Mount Ida, from temple E.*

island was then made into a Province, with a Praetor in Syracuse and two Quaestors, one in Syracuse and the other at Lilybaeum. Sicilian agriculture was strongly developed under Roman rule, and the island enjoyed a period of peace which lasted for centuries. It later passed under the jurisdiction of the Eastern Roman Empire, and a new era of peace began, with the introduction of the Christian faith and of Byzantine culture. In 827, however, the island was invaded by the Saracens, who imposed their iron rule. During the second half of the 11C, a Christian army led by Robert "the Guiscard" and his brother Roger I of Hauteville, who had been mandated by the Pope in Rome, freed the island from Arab control. In 1130 the Kingdom of Sicily was created and, at Christmas that same year, Roger II of Hauteville was proclaimed first King of Sicily. He extended the Sicilian dominion, creating a vast kingdom which stretched from Montecassino to Albania and the North African coasts of Tunisia and Libya. The Hauteville dynasty gave another two great sovereigns to Sicily, William I and his son William II. Men of science and letters, politicians and artists from all over the world gathered at Palermo's court, turning it into a magnificent centre of international culture. After the death of William II, in 1189, the Hauteville dynasty was replaced by that of the Hohenstaufens. The short and tragic reign of Henry VI was followed by a return to ancient splendour in 1208, with the accession to the throne of Henry's son, the great Frederick (I of Sicily; II of the Empire). A great statesman, well-versed in administration, natural science and mathematics, he promoted the development of a new, pre-Renaissance culture at his court. On his death (1250), a period of political unrest began. The crown of Sicily (a vassal of the Holy See) was assigned by the Pope to Charles of Anjou, the brother of the King of France. The Angevins (French) went so far as to subject Sicily to military occupation. This led to the Vespers Revolution, which broke out in Palermo on Easter Monday 1282, causing the expulsion of the Angevins from the island. The legitimate heir to the throne was King Peter of Aragon who, supported by the Sicilian nobility, was crowned King of Sicily in Palermo on 4 September 1282. With the only exception of Frederick II of Sicily, the Aragonese dynasty of Sicily (Crown of Trinacria), which had replaced the Angevins (supported by France), proved to be weak. In the 14C, in fact, the great aristocratic families gained effective control of the island thanks to their economic and military power. The most important – the Alagona, Peralta, Ventimiglia and Chiaramonte families – as a matter of fact divided Sicily into four spheres of influence. This was the period of the four Vicars. In 1392 – after about one century of political weakness on the part of the Crown of Trinacria, and after the doubtful outcome of the Vespers War against the Angevins of Naples (they maintained the title of Kings of Sicily) – the Aragonese of Spain strongly repressed Sicilian aspirations to autonomy. In 1415, Sicily was joined to the Crown of Aragon and was thus ruled by Viceroys. In the 15C King Alfonso "the Magnanimous" (of Aragon and Sicily) managed to reunite the two parts of the ancient State (Sicily and southern Italy), which he refounded as the Kingdom of the two Sicilies. France fomented a series of revolts, which broke out between the 16C and the 17C. In 1672, during the war against Spain, Messina eventually rose up in arms, openly supported by the France of Louis XIV. But, in spite of their victories at sea and on land, in 1678 the French abandoned Augusta and Messina; the latter was severely punished by the Crown, and thus entered an irresistible process of decline. At the beginning of the 18C, Sicily was involved in the Spanish and Polish wars of succession (1700-1738). During a thirty-year period, the island was forced to yield its crown first to the Savoy dynasty, then to the Emperor of Austria Charles VI and, finally, to the Spanish Charles of Bourbon, who began the dynasty of the Bourbons of Naples and restored the autonomy of the Kingdom of Naples and Sicily. Due to the French invasion, King Ferdinand of Bourbon moved to Palermo for a few years. Here he had to yield to the aspirations to autonomy of the aristocracy by promulgating a Constitution (1812). However, when monarchic authority was restored in 1816, he repudiated the Constitution and dissolved the

Siculo-Punic silver tetradachm.

Sicilian Parliament. In 1820-21 the first anti-Bourbon uprising broke out. During the Revolution of 1848, the supporters of the cause of independence created an autonomous Parliament in Naples, and later proposed that an independent Sicily and the other Italian States should join to form a federation. The Revolution was put down by military force. The war of 1860-61 eventually ended with the annexation of Sicily and southern Italy to the Kingdom of Italy, ruled by the House of Savoy. On 15 May 1946, a legislative decree granted regional autonomy to Sicily on the basis of a special Statute. In April 1947, the first Sicilian Regional Parliament was appointed.

Art. The imposing architectural remains of temples, theatres and aqueducts which still rise majestically on the sites of great ancient cities, as well as the large number of fine sculptures, decorative features of ancient buildings, pottery and precious items displayed in the main archaeological museums in Sicily, all bear witness to centuries of Graeco-Sicel, Roman and Byzantine culture, making up one of the most remarkable archaeological treasures of all mankind. The temples of Segesta, Selinunte and Agrigento, the theatres of Taormina, Syracuse and Selinunte, the aqueducts of Termini and Agrigento, the defensive works of Syracuse (the Castle of Euryalus), the archaeological museums in Syracuse, Palermo, Trapani, Himera, etc., as well as the vast archaeological sites of ancient cities such as Agrigento, Heraclea Minoa, Himera, Segesta, Selinunte, etc., cannot be easily summarized here. For brevity's sake, we can say that Sicilian art of antiquity was characterized by the presence of majestic architectural works in cities which astonished the Ancient World with their dimensions. Characteristic features of this art were the highly-developed technical skills (particularly in the field of water-conveying systems), the magnificence of the Roman patrician villas, the refined statuary and the richness and realism of the great mosaic cycles. All these features flourished again both under the Byzantines and in the Middle Ages, when the rest of western Europe was still struggling to free itself from a semi-barbarian condition. Sicilian medieval art in the first decades of the Kingdom (from the end of the 11C through the 12C) was characterized by the fact that almost all the works were commissioned and financed by the Crown. Thanks to their prerogatives as "papal legates", the members of the Hauteville dynasty were able to build the first great Latin cathedrals (Messina; Lipari; Cefalù; Monreale; Catania; Mazara; Agrigento; etc.). In these churches, the new Latin architectural spatiality imported from central Italy and northern Europe combined with the sumptuous decoration from the Maghreb, with the narrative schemes of Byzantine mosaics, and with Apulian Romanesque sculpture. Roger II built Cefalù Cathedral, where he wished to be buried. Later, he had his Royal Palace erected in Palermo, with his own Palace Chapel (the "Palatine Chapel"), the most magnificent example of Sicilian medieval art, built in 1132 and dedicated to St Peter. The Royal Palace also housed the royal art and crafts workshops, where crowns, jewels, precious furnishings and ceremonial clothes were made. Some of these can still be admired today, such as the splendid Byzantine imperial crown *(Kamelaukion)* now displayed in the Cathedral Treasury. Roger II was succeeded by William I, who built the Zisa royal residence within the great royal park. His son, William II, built the Cuba and the majestic Monreale Cathedral, another jewel of royal art. The interior is richly decorated with splendid Byzantine mosaics, and the cloister is one of the most elegant expressions of medieval sculpture applied to architecture. In the meantime, the old Palermo Cathedral was partially demolished and reconstructed as a much larger building on the initiative of Bishop Gualtiero, who transformed it into the greatest cathedral of medieval Sicily. The age of Emperor Frederick II Hohenstaufen was mainly characterized by the building of his castles, which represent a *"unicum"* in world history. The residential needs of the sovereign and defensive needs were combined and satisfied in constructions of refined formal elegance: Castello Ursino (Catania); Castello Maniace (Syracuse) and the Castles of Augusta and Milazzo, as well as the Towers of Enna, of the Colombaia in Trapani, and of Gela. In the

Syracuse Archaeological Museum:
Terracotta lion from the Giardino Spagna
necropolis (7C BC), a perfume receptacle of
Corinthian make.

14C, due to the Vespers War and to Baronial Anarchy, Sicily withdrew into itself, and the art it produced was a mere continuation of the expressive forms which had characterized the previous age. In the 15C, however, the first step was taken towards a new aesthetic taste. The most outstanding figure in architecture was Matteo Carnelivari of Noto, who was active in Palermo towards the end of the century (Palazzo Abatellis, Palazzo Aiutamicristo and the church of Santa Maria della Catena). Antonello da Messina (1430-1479) is the greatest Sicilian painter of all time, and one of the greatest 15C masters in Europe. Some of his paintings have remained in Sicily: the *Portrait of an Unknown Seaman*, in the Cefalù Mandralisca Museum, the *Three Saints* and the splendid *Annunziata* in the Palermo Gallery, the *San Gregorio* polyptych in the Messina Museum, and the *Annunciation* in the Palazzo Bellomo Museum in Syracuse. In sculpture, the most outstanding figure was Domenico Gagini (Bissone c 1420 – Palermo 1492), the founder of a workshop which, for many generations, held a prominent position in the field. In the 16C, the expressive forms of Tuscan and Roman Mannerism began to gain ground. The leading figures were: Antonello Gagini (1478-1536) and Polidoro da Caravaggio (the author of two fine lateral doors in the Duomo of Messina). When Antonello died, his work was continued by his sons. Many Tuscan sculptors moved to Sicily during the 16C, including Montorsoli (famous for the fountains of Orion and Neptune; the *Scylla*, now in the Messina Museum). Among his disciples were Martino Montanini and A. Calamech. In architecture, the forms of Mannerism became popular in the first half of the 17C. Examples of this are, in Palermo: the Quattro Canti (Giulio Lasso); Porta Felice (Pietro Novelli); the churches of Olivella and San Domenico; the old Shipyard (Mariano Smiriglio); the church of the Teatini (Giacomo Besio). And also: the Town Hall in Syracuse (G. Vermexio); the Benedectine Monastery in Catania (V. De Franchis); the College and Church of the Jesuits in Trapani (N. Masuccio). Baroque art was inaugurated by the church of the Annunziata dei Teatini in Messina (Guarino Guarini). It took more austere forms in Palermo with Paolo Amato (1634-1714): Church of the Salvatore; and Giacomo Amato (1643-1732): Church of the Pietà and Santa Teresa alla Kalsa. The famous Villas of Bagheria are a case apart: here the architects' creativity is reflected in the scenographic architectural design and sinuous external staircases (Villa Palagonia; Villa Valguarnera; etc., 18C). More fanciful Baroque forms characterize the towns rebuilt after the 1693 earthquake (Catania, Syracuse, Noto, Grammichele, Avola, Ragusa, Modica, etc.). The Palermitan Vaccarini planned the reconstruction work in Catania (façade of the Cathedral; Palazzo Valle; the Town Hall; St Agatha's Abbey). Rosario Gagliardi (1726-1770) was active in different centres: Noto, Ragusa, Comiso, Caltagirone. His works include the churches of San Domenico and of the Collegio (Noto), those of San Giorgio and San Giuseppe (Ragusa) and the Cathedral of Modica. All these works are characterized by plastic structures and dynamic and original outlines. In painting, the most outstanding figure was P. Novelli of Monreale (1603-1647). His works include the paintings in the Capuchin churches at Ragusa and Leonforte, a large painting in Monreale, and a *St Christopher* in the Catania Museum. Vito D'Anna (1720-1769) can be considered the founder of the school of Sicilian fresco painters of the second half of the century. In sculpture, Giacomo Serpotta (1656-1732) occupies a place of his own. The descendant of a family of sculptors and plastic artists, he was active in Palermo, where he decorated with joyful stuccoes a large number of churches and oratories (Oratories of San Lorenzo, Santa Cita, etc.). Another great sculptor and plastic artist was Ignazio Marabitti (1719-1797) (marble altarpiece of the *Apotheosis of St Benedict* in Monreale Cathedral). 19C architecture began with the neoclassical work of the Palermitan G. V. Marvuglia (1729-1814), including the Oratory of San Filippo Neri all'Olivella and Villa Belmonte, in the Acquasanta quarter (Palermo). The most outstanding figures of late-19C architecture were the Palermitans G. B. F. Basile (Teatro Massimo) and G. Damiani Almeyda (Politeama Garibaldi). The period between

Silver tetradachm from Naxos.

the 19C and the 20C was dominated by the architect Ernesto Basile, a talented designer who introduced a refined and independent Sicilian Liberty style, a forerunner of Rationalism. Among his disciples were several distinguished architects.

Traditions. Sicily still retains some of its age-old traditions both in the working and social fields. Tunny fishing, for example, still uses the traditional techniques ("tonnare"), as does swordfish fishing in the Strait of Messina. The production of ceramic articles is still considerable. Excellent Sicilian wines are still appreciated worldwide. Among local religious cults, the celebrations in honour of the patron saints are of particular interest. The most famous of these is the so-called *Festino* of St Rosalia in Palermo (13-15 July), characterized by the Processions of the Triumphal Chariot and of the silver urn of the *Santuzza,* as Palermitans call their patron saint. Messina celebrates the feast of the Mid-August Madonna (15 August) with the procession of the *vara* (processional bier) of Our Lady of the Assumption and of the two Giants on horseback, the mythical forefathers of the people of Messina. Catania celebrates St Agatha, the patron saint, by carrying her reliquary laden with precious objects through the city streets, pulled by dozens of believers wearing the traditional white "sackcloth" (in February). But the scenographic forms taken by these festivals are innumerable, and each town and village in Sicily has its own. Besides local saints' festivals, the religious celebrations of the Holy Week are also of deep significance for Sicilian people. Particularly suggestive are those held in Enna, Caltanissetta and Trapani. A cycle of celebrations with different characteristics is that of the Byzantine Holy Week at Piana degli Albanesi.

PALERMO

The name Palermo derives from the Greek word *Panormos,* meaning "all port". In fact, it was the spacious natural harbour that favoured the earliest settlements and the founding of the city on an oblong rocky spur bounded to the north by the Papireto River and to the south by the Kemonia. The ancient port, of which only the present-day Cala remains, lays between the mouths of the two rivers. Evidence exists of the presence of different peoples in the area: the Sicans in the 12C BC, followed by the Cypriots, Cretans, Elymi and Greeks. The first permanent urban settlement, however, was founded by the Phoenicians between the 8C and the 7C BC. The *Paleapolis* (from the Greek "old city") lays on the upper part of the oblong rocky spur and was surrounded by strong city walls. A second city, the *Neapolis* (from the Greek "new city"), was later built between the two rivers, but outside the city walls and closer to the port. Between 485 BC and 306 BC Panormos was involved in the long-lasting struggle for supremacy between the Greeks and Carthaginians. From 254 BC, the city was ruled by the Romans. Christianity soon flourished and spread, as is witnessed by the presence of a series of catacombs, including the famous ones of the Papireto (Porta d'Ossuna). In 536, the Gothic garrison which had occupied the city was driven out by the Byzantine general Belisarius, and Palermo passed under the rule of Constantinople, which had re-united the Roman Empire. The first Cathedral was built between 590 and 604 on the initiative of Bishop Victor. Two Palermitans, Agatho and Sergius, became Roman Popes and were later canonized. The city was stormed by the Saracens in 831, after a one-year heroic resistance.

In 1072, Palermo was liberated by a Christian army led by the Hauteville brothers, Roger (Great Count of Sicily) and Robert ("the Guiscard"), and regained its ancient splendour. In 1130, in fact, it became the capital of the Kingdom of Sicily and on Christmas Day that same year the first king, Roger II of Hauteville, was crowned in the Cathedral, which was restored to the Christian cult. Trade and cultural activities had already recovered and were flourishing again, favoured by Palermo's position as the capital of a great cosmopolitan kingdom. Roger II added architectural splendour to the *Castrum superius,* which became his Royal Palace. Inside this complex construction, in 1132, he built his Palace chapel (the "Palatine Chapel"), dedicated to St Peter, which is the most magnificent example of medieval art in Palermo. Meanwhile, the city was enriched with splendid buildings: the churches of San Giovanni dei Lebbrosi, San Giovanni degli Eremiti, San Cataldo, Santa Maria dell'Ammiraglio (the "Martorana"). Just outside the city walls, Roger II created a large park with woods, plantations, stock farms, artificial lakes and luxury royal residences: Maredolce, Favara, Parco (Altofonte). Roger II was suceeded by William I, who built the Zisa royal residence within the great Royal Park. His successor, William II, built the Cuba. During his reign the Hauteville dynasty reached the height of international prestige. He promoted the construction, within the boundaries of the Royal Park, of the great Monreale Cathedral and of the nearby Benedictine monastery and Royal Palace. The church is another gem of medieval architecture in Sicily. The interior is richly decorated with splendid Byzantine mosaics and the cloister is one of the highest expressions of Romanesque sculpture applied to architecture. In the meantime, from 1170 to 1184, the old Palermo Cathedral was partially demolished and reconstructed as a much larger building on the initiative of Bishop Gualtiero, who transformed it into the greatest cathedral of medieval Sicily. In the 12C, Palermo was the splendid capital of the first Italian unitary State after the collapse of the Western Roman Empire.

The Hauteville dynasty was followed by that of the Hohenstaufens, with Emperors Henry VI and Frederick II. The reign of Frederick II was of no advantage to Palermo. On his death (1250), a period of political unrest began, which certainly did not benefit the city. Palermo thus started to slowly lose its role of predominance, while Naples was gradually increasing its prestige. The crown of Sicily (a vassal of the Holy See) was assigned by the Pope to Charles of Anjou, the brother of the King of France. The Angevins (French) went so far as to subject Sicily to military occupation. This led to the "Vespers Revolution", which broke out in Palermo on Easter Monday 1282, causing the expulsion of the Angevins from the island. The legitimate heir to the throne was King Peter of Aragon who, supported by the Sicilian nobility, was crowned King of Sicily in Palermo on 4 September 1282. This marked the beginning of the weak dynasty of the Aragonese of Sicily, who became subject to the great aristocratic families. In the 14C Palermo was in fact under the rule of the powerful Chiaramonte family. But, in 1392, the Aragonese of Spain put an end to these aspirations to autonomy. Andrea Chiaramonte, the only one of the four Vicars who resisted the troops of Martin of Aragon, was captured and beheaded in the Piano della Marina, the square overlooked by his sumptuous Palermitan palace, the *Steri*, which can still be admired today. In 1415 the crown of Sicily was joined to the crown of Aragon, and the island was ruled by Viceroys. These alternately resided in the Chiaramonte family's *Steri* or in the Castellammare (the sea castle), and only at a later time, in the 16C, in the ancient Royal Palace. 15C art was characterized by the "Sicilian Gothic" style, bearing Catalan influences. The most outstanding architect of the time was Matteo Carnelivari of Noto, to whom the elegant church of Santa Maria della Catena, in the Cala quarter, has been attributed. Carnelivari also designed Palazzo Abatellis and Palazzo Aiutamicristo (1490), chosen by Charles V and Don John of Austria as their residences in the following century. Between the 15C and the 16C, new impulse was given to Palermitan sculpture by the workshop of the Gagini, a family of skilful sculptors and stucco decorators (Domenico, Antonello and a host of relatives). The Gagini did not confine their work to sculpturing single statues of Madonnas and Saints, but inserted them into magnificent architectural ensembles, enriched with frames, panels, balustrades depicting stories of the Saints and delicate decorative motifs, which embellished church apses and chapels, thus introducing Tuscan Renaissance taste into Palermo.

In the 17C-18C, architectural activity was promoted not only by the city Senate, but also by two important groups of clients: the Aristocracy and the religious Orders. The great aristocratic families built sumptuous palaces which were unequalled in Europe. Palazzo Villafranca, Palazzo

A view of Palermo, lying along the curve of its gulf against the wide background of the famous **"Conca d'Oro"**, and encircled by a ring of mountains. This photograph was taken from the slopes of **Monte Pellegrino**, defined by Goethe as "the most beautiful promontory in the world". With its imposing calcareous rock mass, the mountain dominates the city from a height of 606 m. Monte Pellegrino (known since the earliest times as **"Heirkte"** and later called **"Gebel Grin"** by the Arabs) delimits the gulf of Palermo to the north. From 247 to 244 BC, during the First Punic War, Hamilcar Barca's Carthaginians, entrenched on the mountain, opposed the Roman legions that had conquered Palermo.

Of great prehistoric and geological interest are the caves opening on the sides of the mountain. The so-called **Addaura Caves** contain wall engravings from the Upper Paleolithic representing animal and human figures. In the foreground on the spur of the mountain stands the "Utveggio" castle, built in 1932 as a hotel and recently acquired by the Sicilian Region to house an international management school.

Ugo, Palazzo Belmonte and Palazzo Riso were erected in Piazza Bologni, Palermo's aristocratic showcase. The majestic Palazzo Trabia rose along the Marina promenade. An entire new street, the *Strada Nova* (the present-day Via Maqueda) was started in 1600 to allow the building of new aristocratic palaces (the most important being Palazzo Comitini). At the crossroads of the *Strada Nova* and the *Cassaro* was, and still is, Piazza Vigliena (also known as the Octagon, the Theatre of the Sun, or the Four Corners of the City), the heart of 17C-18C Palermo. The religious Orders entrusted their "architects in cassocks" (who had been the disciples of the masters of Mannerism and Baroque, in Rome) with the design of religious houses, churches, monasteries and convents. All these buildings contributed to Palermo's architectural grandeur: from the Jesuit Casa Professa to San Giuseppe dei Teatini; from Santa Teresa alla Kalsa to San Domenico; from San Francesco Saverio to Sant'Anna. The prevailing style in architecture was, at this time, Mannerism. Baroque taste was only limited to the internal decoration of most of the churches and of some of the palaces. Church interiors, in particular, were sumptuously decorated with polychrome marble inlays, stuccoed human figures and ornamental motifs, skilfully executed ironwork, polychrome floors, not to mention paintings and furnishings. In sculpture, Palermo outclassed the rest of Italy with the greatest stucco decorator of all time: Giacomo Serpotta (1656-1732), the author of the splendid stuccoes in the Oratories of Santa Cita, the Rosario and San Lorenzo. His work was continued by his son Procopio and by numerous disciples. Great names in painting were those of Pietro Novelli (1603-1647), Filippo Paladini, Vito d'Anna and Antonio Grano. At this time, public festivals – both lay and religious – were at the height of their splendour, also thanks to the rich scenographic ensembles, to the external decorations of churches and palaces, to the magnificent Triumphal Chariots of St Rosalia (the city's patron saint) and to the "firework display machines".

Between the 18C and the 19C, the architect Venanzio Marvuglia designed the Riso, Geraci, Costantino and Coglitore Palaces, the Oratory of San Filippo Neri, Villa Belmonte and the Chinese Palace. In the 19C, the architect G. B. Filippo Basile designed the greatest opera house in Italy, the Teatro Massimo, which was commenced in 1875 and completed in 1897, while the engineer Giuseppe Damiani Almeyda designed the Politeama Garibaldi, erected in 1874. Later, thanks to the elegant work of Ernesto Basile, Filippo's son, Palermo became the Italian capital of the *liberty* architectural style. Among his best-known works are: the Villa Igiea Hotel, Villa Florio, the Florio Pavillon, Villa Deliella (no longer extant), Villa Basile, the Kursaal Biondo, the seat of the Cassa di Risparmio, etc. The best painter of the time was Francesco Lojacono; in sculpture, the best-known artist was Mario Rutelli. Meanwhile, Palermo was expanding beyond its ancient walls, onto the area previously used for the great National Exhibition of 1891. The "middle-class" part of the city was thus created. In the 1950s, crowds of people from the neighbouring provinces arrived in Palermo, mostly attracted by the prospects of a job in the regional administration, resulting in an enormous building expansion.

Agrigento National Museum:
Fine lion-head gargoyle.

PALERMO - MONDELLO

Palermitan beach resort par excellance, Mondello extends along a delightful bay, from the foot of Monte Pellegrino to the foot of Monte Gallo. One of the most famous beach resorts in the island, it has experienced a considerable development since the post-war period which, however, has not affected the extensive green areas surrounding private houses, hotels and places of amusement. Many Palermitans have chosen to live in Mondello, a place that can be rightly called a garden city, far from the nearby city's busy traffic. The old fishing village lies at the northern end of the bay, on the site of an ancient "tonnara" (tunny-fishery) whose 15C round tower is still visible. Another coeval watchtower stands aloof on the furthermost spur to the west of the bay. The beginning of the century, when the Belle Epoque was at its height, witnessed the first elite settlements, which would continue throughout the period between the two wars. Of great interest are: Villa Dagnino (1914), Villa Pojero (1915) and the Sea Kursaal (bathing establishment), built in the late floreal style in fashion at the time.

Top: The Sea **Kursaal** and the equipped beach at the centre of the bay, in the area where the most prestigious hotels are found. The photos in these pages have been taken from the carriage road that, offering panoramic views of the sea, takes from Valdesi to the Sanctuary of Santa Rosalia, and then goes down towards Palermo, with a view of the wide gulf of the same name lying between Capo Mongerbino and the by now metropolitan urban area. Opposite, bottom: The long uninterrupted strip of silvery sand stretching as far as the old fishing village. In some caves at the foot of the overhanging walls of Monte Gallo, to the west of the oldest site, remains from the **Upper Paleolithic** have recently been discovered. In the **grotta dei Vitelli** (Cave of Calves), linear wall engravings have been found. An interesting boat trip can be taken to the Capo Gallo lighthouse, from which a peculiar phenomenon can be observed: a **linear engraving** on the rock, **carved by waves** and left uncovered by the raising of the coastal rock wall.

CHURCH OF SANTA MARIA DELL'AMMIRAGLIO, "LA MARTORANA" CHURCH OF SAN CATALDO

The "Martorana" and San Cataldo Norman churches, in the old city centre, are two outstanding religious buildings dating back to 1143 and 1160, respectively. The Martorana was built by Roger II's Admiral (hence the name of the church), George of Antioch. In the course of the centuries, the original structure has undergone considerable demolitions and alterations, particularly in the 16C, when the present Baroque façade was erected. In 1221 it was entrusted to the Greek clergy and then, in 1433, to the Benedictine convent established by the noblewoman Eloisa Martorana in 1194, which explains the additional name given to the church.

The remaining Norman elements are the bell tower, the domed roof and the external walls with blind arcading around the windows. In the photos, mosaics decorating the interior walls of the church. Left: King Roger crowned by Jesus. Top, right: "The Nativity" and "The Passing Away of the Virgin".

SAN GIOVANNI DEI LEBBROSI

One of the oldest Norman churches in Palermo, San Giovanni dei Lebbrosi (St John of the Lepers) was built in 1071 by Roger I. In the following century (c 1150) a leper hospital was attached to it. Arab craftsmen, often employed by the Normans and Swabians to erect their monuments and palaces, took part in its construction. The bell tower, by F. Valenti, was erected during restoration work carried out in 1934. In the garden to the right of the church, which was originally united to it, are the remains of an Arab construction identified as "Iahia's (John's) Castle". The interior of the church is in the basilican style, with a central nave and two aisles divided by columns; it has three apses and is domed.

THE NORMAN ROYAL PALACE AND THE PALATINE CHAPEL

Because of its historical and artistic significance, the Norman Palace is one of the greatest monuments in Palermo. In the 9C, the Arabs structured and fortified the ***"Qasr"*** as a castle, on the site of a pre-existing Punic-Roman stronghold. After 1130 (when Roger II was crowned King of Sicily) the Normans extended and strengthened the original building with towers and bastions, making it the main fortress in the city and a sumptuous royal palace, in which the political and economic life of the State was administered until the death of Frederick II of Swabia. Under Frederick, the Palace also became a centre of civilisation and culture of European dimension. The Palatine Chapel, indeed a religious jewel, was built by Roger II, who wanted it to be incorporated inside the Palace. Begun in 1130, the Chapel was consecrated in 1143 and dedicated to St Peter. From the late 13C, after the end of the Norman-Swabian dynasty, the political and economic life in Sicily began to decline and the Palace lost its importance as a political and administrative centre. In fact, it was abandoned and neglected until the 15C, the only exception being the Palatine Chapel that continued to be looked after by the clergy in charge of it. Under the Spanish viceroys, in the second half of the 16C, the building became once again a royal residence and underwent considerable alterations. The Norman towers were demolished and the present imposing façade was built, together with the spacious internal courtyards: the 17C Maqueda courtyard, in the middle of a triple portico with limestone arches, and the so-called "fountain" courtyard. The most obvious traces of the Norman period are Torre Pisana (the Pisan tower), Roger's Room in the Joaria and the Palatine Chapel. Since the post-war period the Norman Palace has been the seat of the Sicilian Regional Assembly.

*Photos: The present structure of the **Norman Palace** façade. From left to right, the façade of the Palace, built by the Viceroy Vigliena in 1616; **Torre Pisana** and, in the background, the spire of **Porta Nuova** with the Baroque loggia dating from 1669.*

*Right: The portico on the first floor of the **Maqueda courtyard** leading to the **Palatine Chapel**, with Egyptian granite columns, the original external structure of the Chapel.*

This scene from a glittering gilded mosaic depicts the **FLIGHT INTO EGYPT**. The Virgin Mary is riding a white donkey; ahead of her, Joseph is carrying young Jesus on his shoulders, holding his leg, while the young boy is hanging onto his father's hair to keep his balance. Behind them is a figure that the Protevangelium of St James identifies as young James, the child Joseph had from his first marriage, holding a whip in his right hand and a poor bundle in the left.

Below: **THE ENTRY INTO JERUSALEM**. The ancient Greek inscription on the upper side reads "The Palm procession", one among the most significant Christian feasts. On the right side, a group of distinguished figures in a pleased and welcoming attitude, waiting outside the towered city walls with the outline of the buildings. In the middle, the figure of St Peter gesturing with his right hand to invite Jesus, sitting astride a donkey, to enter the city. On the left, the other Apostles follow, in a dignified attitude and aware of the solemnity of the event.

"The Palatine Chapel, the most beautiful in the world, the finest religious jewel ever dreamt of by human thought and executed by the hands of an artist..."
(Guy de Maupassant)

THE PALATINE CHAPEL
"The most perfect work ever produced by Christian art"

Thus commented Augusto Schneegans at the sight of this incomparable monument. Its structure and the interior decorations represent the artistic fusion of the three components - Siculo-Roman, Byzantine and Arab - which have created immortal architectural masterpieces in Sicily. The interior combines the longitudinal plan of a Roman basilica with a central Byzantine body, creating a harmonius conjunction of lines and volumes. It extends over 32 metres lengthwise, with a nave and two aisles divided by two lines of five alternating Egyptian mar-

ble and half-fluted cipolin columns with Corinthian or composite capitals, one of which is Arab. The Chapel is 12.5 m wide and 12.4 m high (18 m in the dome). The wooden lacunar of the nave was executed by Muslim craftsmen and is decorated with figures and inscriptions in Cufic characters. Mosaics entirely cover the walls of the nave, aisles and sanctuary, in a glittering gilded phantasmagoria of biblical scenes, saints and stories from the life of Christ.

*Opposite page, top: Mosaic representation of **Christ Pantocrator** blessing in the central apse. In his left hand, Jesus is holding the Gospel; the Greek and Latin inscription reads: "I am the light of the world. Whoever follows me will never walk in darkness, but will have the light of life".*

Bottom, left: Christ blessing overhanging the royal throne on the back wall. Jesus is sitting on the throne and is flanked by the Apostles Peter and Paul; above them, the Archangels Gabriel and Michael. The two lions at the sides of the throne are a symbol of power and sovereignty.

*Opposite: The solemn figure of **The Virgin Mary with the Holy Child** from the majestic mosaic of the Nativity. The Madonna is holding the Child in her arms, presenting him to the adoring Magi. Above, the Latin inscription reads: "The star begets the sun, the rose begets the flower, form begets beauty".*

Top: The twin-aisled basilican interior with the main apse, the high altar and Christ blessing in the bowl-shaped vault. The walls and vaults of the arches are entirely covered with glittering gilded mosaics depicting the Apostles and Saints, with floreal and geometric decorations.

Above and below: Examples of the splendid mosaic decorations covering the surface of the entire Chapel.

Top: **Christ Pantocrator** with Angels and Archangels, in the bowl-shaped vault of the central cupola. The Greek inscription surrounding the figure of Christ reads: **Heaven is my throne and Earth my footstool, says Christ Pantocrator**.

Bottom, left: Detail of the ceilings of the nave and aisles, with Gothic rosettes, wooden works by Fatimid craftsmen.

Opposite: **The ambo and the Paschal candlestick** - The ambo consists of two cubic bodies in porphyry and marble decorated with fine mosaics. The Paschal candlestick, 4.26 m high, is supposed to date from the mid-12C and to be modelled on the similarly famous Candlestick in the Basilica di San Paolo Fuori le Mura in Rome.

The earliest mosaics in the Chapel, as the Greek inscription on the dome testifies, date from 1143 and reflect the Byzantine mosaic tradition of the 10C and 11C.

The latest, characterized by Latin inscriptions and depicting Stories from the New Testament, are the ones along the nave (1154-68). The mosaics in the two aisles, depicting Stories of St Peter and St Paul, date from the 14C. The crypt is actually a small pre-existing church, on the site of which Roger had the Palatine Chapel built. Recent restoration work has brought to light the sepulchre of William the Bad; the crypt also contains the remains of the Viceroy of Sicily, Emmanuel Filibert of Savoy, who died in 1624.

Above: A view of the Chapel interior from the left aisle, showing the architectural inequality of the columns, with ancient or reproduction shafts and capitals.
Below, left: Detail of the throne, with the precious mosaic marble inlays. Below, right: Christ blessing, with the Gospel opened on the Greek verse: "I am the light of the world. Whoever follows me will never walk in darkness but will have the light of life" (John 8:12).

ROGER'S ROOM

Roger's Room in the Joaria, the part of the Palace where Norman and Swabian kings used to spend long hours of recreation and relax, surrounded by the royal court and by scientists, poets and distinguished men-at-arms and statesmen. Here Frederick II, a poet himself, gathered the most talented personalities of the time, giving impetus to the Sicilian School of Poetry where, as acknowledged by Dante, the first poems in the Italian language were written. The gilded mosaics decorating the room depict figures of birds, swans, peacocks, deer, lions, leopards and centaurs. The fine mosaic cycle was started under Roger but completed during the reign of William I known as the Good.

*Above: The **"Sala dei Venti"** (Room of the Winds), leading to King Roger's Room in the Joaria tower.*
*Below: **"Roger's Room"** with its mosaic decorations, revealing the eastern figurative tradition of Arab craftsmen, who left their evocative artistic and scenographic imprints not only in the Palace but also in the other royal residences scattered across the luxuriant gardens of the "Conca d'Oro" and in the great hunting park wanted by Roger for his and his court's hunting exploits.*

CHRONOLOGY OF THE NORMAN PALACE

7C BC - Punic settlement and fortress (from literary sources and remains of earlier stonework).

254 BC - The fortress is conquered by the Romans.

535 AD - Belisarius conquers the city, which remains for about three centuries under Byzantine rule.

831 - The Arabs conquer Palermo and occupy the Palace, which becomes the Emirs' residence.

1072 - Norman conquest. The fortress becomes the Norman Palace and is transformed and enriched.

1130 - **Roger II** erects the **Palatine Chapel**.

1195 - **Henry IV of Swabia** begins the Swabian dynasty of Sicily.

1220-30 - **Frederick II** founds the **"Sicilian School of Poetry"** in the Palace.

1282 - **Peter of Aragon** occupies the Palace after the expulsion of the Angevins.

Afterwards the Normal Palace is only discontinuously inhabited by the Viceroys. After 1500 it undergoes considerable restoration work and alterations, up to the expulsion of the Bourbons in 1799.

Photos: The refined mosaic wall-decorations in Roger's Room.
Allegorical peacocks on an arabesqued background. Snow-white swans wandering through the palms and the luxuriant vegetation. The ceiling depicting wild beasts and the Norman eagle standing out in the middle of the mosaic motif.

Above: Deer hunters shooting their arrows. Lions fought with palms, a Sassanid motif introduced by the Arabs.
Below: Centaurs fighting, about to shoot their arrows. Spotted leopards and many-coloured birds surrounded by a luxuriant date palm vegetation, an Oriental-inspired motif.

On these pages, details of the mosaic decoration in Roger's Room testifying to the splendour of Norman civilisation, whose forms and decorations were influenced by Arab-Byzantine tradition. The Norman and Swabian political dream, imbued with scientific and poetic values, took shape in these rooms. Here Frederick II matured into an enlightened emperor, a poet and writer himself, surrounded by the most talented personalities of the time.

SAN GIOVANNI DEGLI EREMITI

One of the best known Norman monuments, the church of San Giovanni degli Eremiti was built by Roger II in 1136, on the site of a pre-existing Gregorian monastery. The clean-cut square building, with domes standing out above it, is clearly a Muslim element (*the qubba*), of which other architectural examples exist in Palermo, testifying to the employment of Arab craftsmen for its construction. The small late-Norman cloister, with an Arab cistern in the middle, was part of the original Benedectine monastery; it has little round arches supported by fine paired columns.

THE "ZISA"

"Whenever you want, you'll see the finest possession
Of the most splendid kingdom in the world: the seas,
And the mountain that (dominates) them, whose peaks are tinged with nar-
cissus and
....
You'll see the (seed)ing of the furrow in the lovely scene
(which) magnificence and happiness befit
This is the Garden of Eden coming into sight;
This is the Mosta'izz (desirous of glory, as William II wanted to be called)
and this (palace),"Aziz".

This Arabic epigraph, translated into Italian by the Palermitan historian Michele Amari, author of a volume on the history of the Muslims in Sicily ("Storia dei Mussulmani in Sicilia"), attests to the derivation of the name of the palace from the Arabic word "Aziz", meaning "splendid". The gilded stucco inscription, written on a cornice along the top of the building, was removed in the 16C to make room for the merlons that are visible today. The original structure has undergone various adaptations and alterations. The double-light windows of the higher orders have been removed, and the interiors have been re-arranged several times. The palace, which was the seasonal residence of Norman sovereigns, was built by William I and completed by his son William II between 1165 and 1167.

Top: The huge clean-cut structure of the rectangular building, with the three barrel-vaults and the blind arches that framed the double-light windows. Bottom: The mosaic-decorated fountain room, where the water supplying the external basin (a fish vivarium) used to spring.

THE CATHEDRAL

This magnificent and imposing religious building was erected on the site of the old cathedral, built by St Gregory the Great in 603, transformed into a mosque by the Arabs and reconsecrated to the Christian cult by the Norman kings. The present building was founded by Gualtiero Offamilio (Walter of the Mill), Archbishop of Palermo from 1168 to 1193, during the reign of the Norman king William II, known as the Good. Even though the original structures have remained unaltered throughout the centuries, the construction underwent several additions and alterations between the 14C and the 16C. Between 1781 and 1801 the architect Ferdinando Fuga transformed the Latin-cross basilican plan adding the side aisles, the wings of the transept and the majestic dome. Since the days of its construction, the Cathedral has witnessed some of the most important events in the history of the city and of the entire island. Here the Norman and Swabian kings were crowned and buried in the Imperial Tombs. Here, in the Santa Rosalia Chapel, the relics of the patron saint of the city are contained in a sumptuous silver urn.

*Top: Constance of Aragon's **gold tiara**, decorated with gems, enamels and pearls, was found in her sepulchre and exhibited in the Treasury showcases.*
Bottom: The southern portico, a splendid example of Gothic-Catalan style, was built in 1430 by Antonio Gambara as was the portal, closed by wooden doors carved by Francesco Miranda in 1432.
Following pages: A view of the southern front of the Cathedral, bearing the traces of the original Norman architecture over the 18C small domes.

+ SICANIE·REGINA·FVI·CONSTANTIA·CONIVNX·
AVGVSTA·HIC·HABITO·NVNC·FEDERICE·TVA·

The interior of the Cathedral was transformed between 1781 and 1801 and given its present neoclassical appearance. It has a Latin-cross basilican plan, with a nave and two aisles divided by pillars; the archivolted interior incorporates granite columns from the pre-existing church. The nave is covered by a bright barrel vault and flanked by a row of marble statues of Saints placed on each pillar and in the transept.

THE IMPERIAL AND ROYAL TOMBS

Top: The Roman sarcophage, decorated with hunting scenes, containing the mortal remains of Constance of Aragon, Frederick II's wife, who died in 1222. Bottom, from left to right: Three monumental tombs containing the mortal remains of Frederick II (d. 1250), Roger II (d. 1154) and his daughter the Empress Constance (d. 1198).

THE SANCTUARY OF SANTA ROSALIA

The veneration of this solemn and grave woman figure by the people of Palermo can be traced back to the 17C, when a hunter accidentally found the Saint's bones in a cave, on 15 July 1625. St Rosalia was born c 1132 from count Sinibaldo della Quisquinia and Mary Guiscard, related to Roger II. At the age of 18, she was introduced to the Norman court as a maid of honour of Marguerite of Navarre, William I's wife. Her family was ruined as a consequence of an anti-royal plot brought forth by the aristocracy, led by Admiral Matteo Bonello, lord of Caccamo, and bloodily repressed by the sovereign after the assassination of his minister Maione di Bari.

Rosalia's father, count Sinibaldo, who had taken part in the plot, was killed and the family property confiscated; as the rebellion was subdued, in 1161, Rosalia definitively consecrated her life to Jesus and lived as a hermit in a cave on Monte Pellegrino till her death on 4 September 1166. In 1625 a violent epidemic of plague struck Palermo, and the Saint's relics were carried in procession through the city, causing the immediate end of the scourge. Every year, from 13 to 15 July, the Palermitans arrange a three-day celebration to thank St Rosalia for the miracle, renewing the traditional devotion to their venerated patron Saint.

*Top: The statue of **St Rosalia**, donated by King Charles III of Bourbon, lying under a baldachin, clothed in a gilded silver mantle and surrounded by a host of votive offerings. Left: The 17C façade of the Sanctuary, placed at a height of 429 m on the mountainside, near the cave in which St Rosalia lived her hermit's life.*

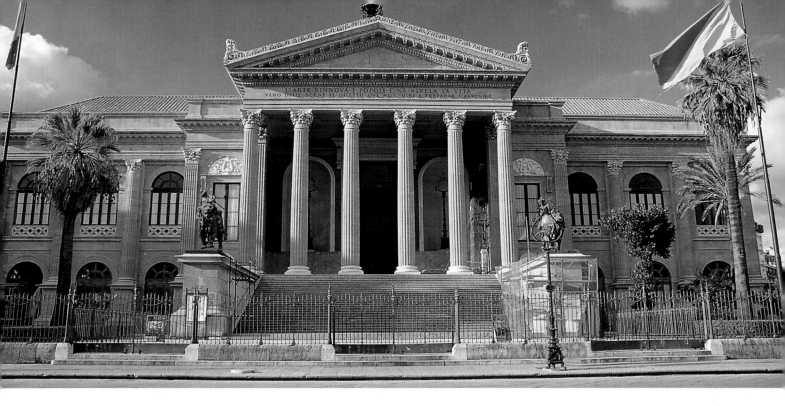

TEATRO MASSIMO

This noble building, the foremost opera house in Palermo, was started in 1875 by G.B. Basile and completed by his son Ernesto in 1897. Regarded as one of the largest theatres in Europe, covering an area of 7,730 sq m, it was decorated and embellished by a large number of artists including the sculptors B. Civiletti, M. Rutelli and A. Ugo. The stage curtain was painted by G. Sciuti and depicts Roger the Norman parading on the day of his coronation. The vast and magnificent hall (450 sq m) has a gallery and five orders of boxes for a total of 3,200 seats.

TEATRO AND PIAZZA POLITEAMA

The theatre was built by Giuseppe Damiani Almeyda between 1867 and 1874; its neoclassical style is influenced by Pompeiian architecture, with curved surfaces and superimposed ambulatories adorned with a double order of Doric and Ionic columns. The curved façade is broken by a protruding body forming a triumphal arch. On the top of the building, the spectacular bronze high-relief by Mario Rutelli, a quadriga flanked by two genii on horseback.

PALAZZINA CINESE

Situated in the middle of the large Favorita park, the "Chinese Palace" was built for King Ferdinand III of Bourbon by Venanzio Marvuglia in 1799. It is characterized by a peculiar combination of different styles, including a neoclassical structure enriched with Chinese motifs as well as Gothic elements.
During Ferdinand IV's forced stay in Palermo, it became the favourite residence of the king and of his wife Maria Carolina; it also housed Admiral Nelson and Lady Hamilton. The vaulted ceilings were decorated with frescoes by G. Patania and V. Riolo. In the basement are the dance-hall and the royal audience hall in Louis XVI style. Upstairs are the hall of representation and the dining-room, whose table is equipped with a peculiar device to serve the courses and change the dishes without the servants' help. To the left of the building is the "royal chapel", built in neoclassical style with an octagonal plan and a dome supported by eight Ionic marble columns; above the altar is a large painting of the **"Madonna della Lettera"**. Of great interest is a visit to the **"Pitrè Ethnographic Museum"** (Museo Etnografico Siciliano Pitrè), one of the most important in Europe, founded by the Palermitan ethnologist Giuseppe Pitrè in 1909. Its rich collection documents Sicilian life, usages and customs.

PORTA NUOVA

The present-day monument was built in 1583 on the site of a pre-existing 15C construction, to celebrate the arrival in Palermo of Charles V of Habsburg, Emperor and King of Sicily, after his victory in Tunis against the Ottoman Turks, in 1535. Situated about halfway along the straight-lined Cassaro, the main thoroughfare of the old Punic-Roman settlement, it has a double monumental façade in Manneristic style with a wide barrel-vault, a small loggia and a majolica-tiled pinnacle.

PORTA FELICE

This majestic monument, erected in 1582 by the Viceroy Marcantonio Colonna, was named after his wife, donna Felice Orsini. Situated at the beginning of the Cassaro, opposite and symmetrical to Porta Nuova, it gives access to the city from the seaside and was built to celebrate the completion of the new 17C artery. Its construction was interrupted in 1584 due to the Viceroy's departure and completed in 1637 by the architects Mariano Smiriglio, Vincenzo Tedeschi and Pietro Novelli.

THE CAPUCHIN CATACOMBS

The crypts of the Capuchin convent, built in 1621, house the world-famous "Catacombe dei Cappuccini".
The place, indeed offering quite a macabre sight, displays the mummified or embalmed corpses of wealthy Palermitans (including women and children) and clergymen, buried there until 1881, when the custom was abolished.
In the adjoining graveyard is the tomb of G. Tomasi di Lampedusa, author of the famous novel "The Leopard".

Photos: Four images of the mummified corpses in the "Capuchin Catacombs".

PIAZZA PRETORIA

One of the scenographic urban areas of the old city centre, the square is dominated by domes and, on its sides, by two great religious buildings, facing each other on its east-west axis. To the east of the square is the **church of Santa Caterina**, attached to an important Dominican monastery with a large cloister housing a fountain with the statue of St Dominic, by Ignazio Marabitti. Erected between 1580 and 1596 in late-Renaissance style, the façade is on two orders and is adorned with pilaster strips, trabeations, and a fine Gaginesque portal. The imposing dome dates back to the 18C. To the west of the square is the side of the church of **San Giuseppe dei Teatini**, with the slender dome adorned by paired columns in the drum and the polychrome majolica-tiled calotta. The church, designed by the Theatine Giacomo Besio, was started in 1612 and completed in 1645. On the southern side stands the Senatorial Palace, now the Town Hall, generally known as Palazzo delle Aquile, erected in 1463 and then enlarged and restored on various occasions until 1823. The magnificent circular fountain, nearly occupying the entire square, was built by the Florentine Francesco Camillani for the Florentine villa of don Pietro di Toledo and resold to the city of Palermo in 1573. On the left, two of the fascinating groups of statues adorning the fountain, with allegorical figures, pagan divinities, hermae and animal heads.

THE SICILIAN REGIONAL GALLERY
AND THE ARCHAEOLOGICAL MUSEUM

The Sicilian Regional Gallery (Galleria Regionale della Sicilia) is housed in Palazzo Abatellis, built in 1490-95 by Matteo Carnelivari in late Gothic-Catalan forms with Renaissance influences. The sumptuous residence was commissioned by Francesco Abatellis, the royal "pretore" (magistrate) of Palermo, and his wife Eleonora Soler. The building was seriously damaged during World War II and restored in 1954 by Carlo Scarpa. Its rooms house an important collection of sculptures and paintings by renowned Sicilian and European artists, particularly from the 14C and 16C. The entrance and courtyard rooms display sculptures from different ages and by different artists, statues, stonework and pottery, architectural fragments and the coat of arms of the Abatellis as well as of other Sicilian noble families. The Museum has sixteen exhibition rooms which alternately display painting and sculpture masterpieces, including the works of such great painters and sculptors as

Francesco Laurana, *Antonello da Messina*, *Antonello Gagini* and his school, *Domenico Gagini*, *Serpotta* and other renowned artists.

For its vast collection of Greek and Roman works, the Regional Archaeological Museum (Museo Archeologico Regionale) is one of the foremost archaeological museums in Italy.

It is housed in the *former Olivella monastery*, attached to the church of Sant'Ignazio all'Olivella, built between 1598 and 1622 to a design by Antonio Muttone, with a magnificent 17C Baroque façade adorned with three portals. The exhibition rooms are arranged on the three floors of the former monastery belonging to St Philip's Congregation, with a succession of archaeological finds, sculptures, collections of vases, coins and epigraphs that span the millennia, from the Phoenician civilisation to the Greek colonization and the Roman Age, documenting Sicily's noble past.

*Above: The **"Malvagna Triptyc"** (1510) depicting the Virgin enthroned with Child and angels, by the Dutch painter Ian Gossaert, known as* **Mabuse**.

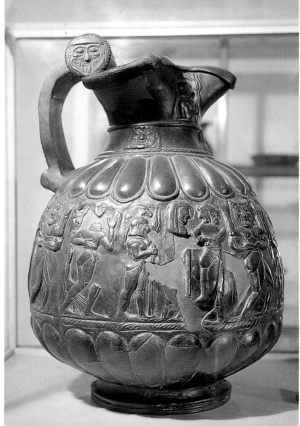

Top: Bronze Room: **"Hercules killing a deer"**, originally part of a bronze group adorning a fountain in the peristyle of a Pompeiian house.
Bottom, left: Etruscan Collection Rooms with finds from Chiusi. Large bucchero **"oinochoe"** with figured relief decoration (mid-6C BC).
Right: Hollow cinerary statue (5C BC) depicting a woman figure enthroned with a pomegranate in her left hand.

Regional Gallery: On the left, the famous **"Bust of Eleanor of Aragon"** by **Francesco Laurana**, Dalmatian sculptor and medallist from Zara (1425-c1502). The splendid and proud marble bust of the Spanish infanta, smooth and curved and wrapped in a thin damask cloth, conveys the pursuit of almost geometric volumes, pervaded with a refined intellectual stylization.

Below: On the back wall of the Palazzo Abatellis chapel is the magnificent fresco with the **"Triumph of Death"**, formerly in Palazzo Sclafani in Palermo, dating from the mid-15C. The riding Death strikes the powerful and the Epicurean youth, sparing the crippled and the beggars. The fresco, formerly attributed to a Catalan painter, is now regarded as a Gothic work, perhaps attributable to the school of Pisanello, a Veronese painter (Antonio Pisano 1397 ? - 1455, known as Pisanello since he was the son of a Pisan draper).

Right: **"Our Lady of the Annunciation"**: one of the finest works by Antonello da Messina, painted in 1473. The brightness of its colours - the blue of the mantle, the pale brown of the complexion, the yellow of the pulpit - is remarkable. The purity of contour of the oval face is enhanced by the mantle framing it. The date of birth of **Antonello da Messina**, the greatest and most famous Sicilian painter, is uncertain. Based on Vasari's assumption that Antonello died in 1479 at the age of 39, the artist was born in Messina in 1430 from Giovanni Michele de Antonio "mazono", i.e. stone- or marble-cutter (derived from the medieval meaning of the French word "maçon"), and Garita, probably the short version of Margherita. From a letter written by Summonte we learn that Antonello joined Colantonio's school in Naples from 1445 to 1455. Antonello's works are now exhibited in various European and North-American museums.

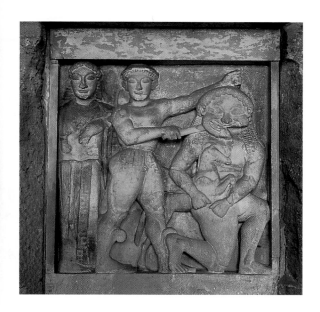

Top, left: **Etruscan Collection Room**. *Rectangular sarcophagi with the half-lying figure of the deceased depicted on the lid and relief mythological figures adorning the coffin.*

Bottom, left: The fine bronze **"Ram"** *which adorned the portal of the Maniace castle in Syracuse until 1040. Its pair was destroyed by a cannon shot during the 1848 revolution.*

Selinunte Room: *Two metopes from the temples of Selinunte. Above:* **Perseus killing the Gorgon assisted by Athena**, *from the pronaos of* **Temple C**.

Below: Metope from **Temple E** *with* **Hera presenting herself to Zeus on Mount Ida**.

Right: The **"Ephebus of Selinunte"** *(5C BC), a Greek bronze statue showing indigenous influences.*

MONREALE CATHEDRAL - "The most beautiful Temple in the world"

The Cathedral stands aloof on the edge of the historical centre of Monreale, a small town overlooking the Oreto River valley and the famous "Conca d'Oro". "The golden temple", a fairy-tale construction, the Christian apotheosis of a Norman king's dream: one morning of 1174, William II, known as "the Good", Roger II's grandson and third Norman King of Sicily, awoke early at daybreak and told his ministers he had dreamt of the Virgin Mary asking him to build her a church with the treasure stolen from the State by his father, William I known as "the Bad", and hidden in a secret place that she would have shown him. Driven by the desire to emulate his grandfather Roger, the founder of the superb Cefalù Cathedral and Palatine Chapel, the king made his dream come true by building a church that equalled, and maybe surpassed, the great Roman and Byzantine Christian cathedrals in artistic and architectural splendour.

We like to believe (and we are sure we are not mistaken) that he was also driven by his religious faith and by his determination to restore Christian tradition in Sicily, after centuries of neglect due to Muslim rule.

*Below: The façade of **Monreale Cathedral**. The massive original towers (the left one is incomplete) flank the 18C portico, adorned with three arches supported by monolithic Doric columns. The marble balaustrade sticks out from the upper section of the façade, decorated with entwined arches divided by the wide central lancet window. (In the foreground) A typical Sicilian cart.*

Right: The main portal. The bronze doors made by Bonanno Pisano (1186) are divided into 42 relief panels depicting scenes from the Bible.

53

In 1174, at the young age of 20, the king began the construction of both the Cathedral and the vast architectural complex including the Benedictine Abbey, the Archbishop Palace and the Royal Palace.

Apart from William's ambition to hand down to posterity his own name and that of his Norman royal house by erecting the magnificent Christian church, this architectural project was thus meant as a testimony to the Christian faith of the young king who, like his predecessors, wanted to assume the Arab title of Caliph under the name of "al-Musta'izz bi-llah", "He who searches exaltation in God". Therefore, political and historical reasons of State inspired the king's profound religious faith. The Latin basilican plan with the Byzantine-type cross vault is not domed and covers a vast area (102 m long and 40 m wide).

It is divided into a nave and twin aisles by 18 columns with capitals of exquisite workmanship, decorated with mosaic-covered pulvinoes (Byzantine transformation of the Greek abacus), clypei of pagan divinities, acanthus leaves and cornucopias overflowing with fruit.

The columns bear Saracen-style pointed arches. The mosaic floor, with granite and porphyry geometric decorations, is the original one completed in the 16C. The walls of the nave, transept and apses are entirely decorated with mosaics on a gilded background, covering a total area of 6,340 sq m.

The mosaic decorations are the work of Byzantine and Venetian craftsmen, executed between the end of the 12C and the beginning of the 13C and depicting a cycle of scenes from the Old and the New Testaments.

*Photo: The three apses of **Monreale Cathedral** (with entwined blind arches supported by small columns and tall piers decorated with polychrome limestone and lava inlays), their architectural and decorative motifs attesting to the large contribution given by Muslim craftsmen to the construction of the majestic building.*

The central apse of the Cathedral, with the huge figure of **Christ Pantocrator** (from the Greek Pantocrator = Almighty). The figures in the apse are arranged according to a logico-hierarchical order, with the figure of Christ in the apsidal vault emphatically dominating the mosaic representation of the Virgin and Child in the middle, flanked by angels and apostles, and figures of saints underneath. The majestic Christ (13.30 m wide and 7 m high) is blessing with his right hand, while his left hand is holding the Gospel, open on the page which reads, in Latin: "I am the light of the world. Whoever follows me will never walk in darkness".

Round his head is a nimbus with a cross, symbol of the Passion. The Virgin is sitting on the throne and holding the blessing Child on her knees, flanked by the Greek inscriptions "Mother of Christ", the assertion of her divine motherhood as defined by the Council of Ephesus, and "All Pure", to signify the "Immaculate Conception" a few centuries before Pope Pius IX's declaration. The apse with the figures of Christ and the Virgin is the focal point and the mystical and religious culmination of the poetic mosaic narration.

THE CLOISTER

This splendid example of Sicilian Romanesque sculpture, almost intact in its original architecture, was built by William II together with the basilica and the Benedictine Monastery, of which it was part. The four sides of the square cloister (each 47 m long) are entirely surrounded by a portico, with an uninterrupted series of 228 small paired columns bearing capitals and pointed arches. This is what a remarkable tourist from the last century, the writer and novelist Guy de Maupassant, wrote about his "Journey to Sicily":

"The marvellous Monreale cloister, instead, conjures up an impression of such grace as to make one want to stay there forever...The exquisite proportions, the incredible slenderness of the light paired columns, one beside the other, all different, some covered with mosaics, others bare; some decorated with sculptures of unmatched delicacy, others adorned with simple stone carvings which wind round them as a creeper, are a wonder to behold, casting spells and generating that artistic joy which, through the eye, penetrates the soul at the sight of such exquisite beauty. How could one not love these cloisters, so steeped in peace, closed and invented, it might seem, with the purpose of generating most profound thoughts as one walks slowly under the arcades! How one feels that these corridors of stone, these corridors of columns enclosing a little garden which rests the eye without disturbing or distracting it, were created to stir one's imagination! One cannot contemplate this genuine masterpiece of beauty and grace without recalling Victor Hugo's verses on the Greek artist who was able to lay

"Something as beautiful as a human smile
On the Propylaea's profile".

The heavenly walk takes place amid high ancient walls with pointed arches, the only remains of the monastery".

(Guy de Maupassant)

*Below: **The Chapel of the Crucifix**, in the left wing of the church. The Spanish Archbishop Giovanni Roano had it erected between 1690 and 1692; it was designed by the Capuchin father Giovanni da Monreale and accomplished by the Jesuit architect Angelo Italia da Licata. This Baroque masterpiece, inlaid with polychrome Sicilian semi-precious stones, was built to house the miraculous Crucifix overhanging the altar which, according to tradition, was donated to the church by King William II. In the lateral niches of the transept, the marble statues of Faith and Hope.*

*Photo: A detail of the square enclosure, surrounded by three arches on each side, known as the **"chiostrino"** (little cloister); in the middle, a Saracen-style fountain in the shape of a stylised palm-tree surmounted by a bud with twelve dancing or playing figures. A circle of twelve lion-heads drop trickles of water into the circular basin underneath, producing a lovely murmur that enhances its subtle charm and fills the heart with such evocative beauty. An unforgettable and emotional visit, imbued with profound religious sentiments.*

Capitals adorning the Monreale Cloister. These masterpieces of Sicilian Romanesque sculpture bear further witness to the employment of Muslim, Greek-Oriental and maybe Provençal craftsmen. All the paired columns on the four sides of the cloister stand on a three-tore plinth encircled by acanthus leaves. The double-faced capitals, surmounted by the abacus, *are characterized by the magnificent plastic representation of human and animal figures. The extremely varied columns are smooth or zigzag-fluted, with glittering mosaic encrustments; others, such as the four corner columns, have relief decorations.*
Above: The Cloister garden.

65

BAGHERIA

The town first developed around the monumental villas built by the Palermo nobility on the gentle hillsides of the Palermitan countryside, facing the sea that surrounds Monte Catalfano and the Aspra promontory. In the 17C, Prince Giuseppe Branciforte built the first Baroque villa, **villa Butera**, and the urban area began to expand along its north-south road axis. Similar villas were built in the following years: **La Cattolica**, **villa Valguarnera** (the most magnificent one, designed by Tommaso Maria Napoli and erected in 1721), **Villarosa**, built in the late 18C and probably designed by Nicolò Palma, and **villa Palagonia** (1715), designed by Tommaso Maria Napoli, the town's most famous construction because of the bizarre figures of monsters decorating the entrances and the fencing wall. Of major architectural interest is the scenographic back of the building (see photo in the middle, opposite page), enlivened by a pincer-shaped staircase of remarkable artistic layout. Interesting frescoes depicting the "Labours of Hercules" decorate the elliptical vestibule on the first floor of the villa.

SOLUNTO

According to Thucydides, Solunto was founded by the Phoenicians together with Motya and Panormo. The Athenian historian refers to it as **Soloeis**, while Diodorus calls the city **Solus**. Cicero writes of its inhabitants referring to the name-place **Solus-Soluntum**. The Punic name, as appears from coin inscriptions, was Kfr = Kafara = village. Excavations have brought to light the city rebuilt on Monte Catalfano around the mid-6C. The older city, mentioned by Thucydides, has not been identified yet, but it probably stood more or less on the same site as the later one.

The city had always been part of the western Carthaginian "epikrateia" until the Roman conquest in 250 BC. At the end of the 2C AD it was voluntarily abandoned by its inhabitants. It was completely destroyed by the Saracens and made uninhabitable during the Muslim rule of the island. The excavations of Soluntum, started in 1826 and resumed in different periods, show the prevalence of Hellenistic and Roman forms in the city plan, with a geometric Hippodameic layout in which the roads parallel to the main thoroughfare were crossed by steep minor roads, often flights of steps.

Left: An example of "domus" revealing its Hellenistic and Roman forms in the "opus signinum" floor.

PORTICELLO AND CAPO ZAFFERANO

The coast stretching from Porticello to San Nicolicchio and Sant'Elia, then continuing to Capo Zafferano and running round the rocky slopes of Monte Catalfano as far as Capo Mongerbino and Aspra, is one of the most picturesque and panoramic stretches of the Palermitan coast. Porticello, an old fishing village, is a popular holiday resort with private houses, hotels and restaurants scattered all along the coast. From Monte Catalfano a magnificent view stretches as far as Capo Plaia and Cefalù and often, on the clearest days, some of the Aeolian islands can be seen. From Aspra there is a fine view of the entire Gulf of Palermo with Monte Pellegrino and Capo Gallo.

*Top: A view of the fishing port of **Porticello** (where pleasure boats are also kept) lying at the foot of **Monte Catalfano** with the remains of the ancient **Solunto**. Bottom: The stretch of coast delimited by the cone-shaped mass of **Capo Zafferano**, offering an interesting itinerary among beautiful landscapes.*

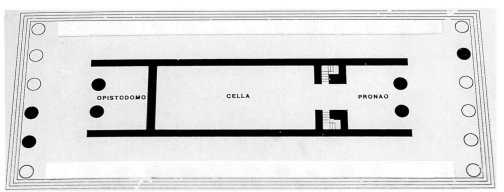

THE BATTLE OF HIMERA

As Herodotus wrote: "...had not Terillus, the son of Crinippus, tyrant of Himera, driven from his city by Theron... King of Agrigentum, brought into Sicily at this very time an army of three hundred thousand men, Phoenicians (Carthaginians), Libyans, Iberians, Ligurians, Helisycians, Sardinians, and Corsicans, under the command of Hamilcar the son of Hanno, King of the Carthaginians..."

Herodotus (VII, 165)

Those were the Punic forces drawn up in battle array.

HIMERA "The Temple of Victory"

In 648 BC a group of Chalcidians from Zancle (Messina), together with inhabitants from Mylai (Milazzo) and Syracusan exiles founded the city of Himera near the river bearing the same name. Lying on a plateau overlooking the valley underneath, facing the Tyrrhenian Sea, Himera was the westernmost Greek city on the northern coast of Sicily. Recent archaeological excavations have brought to light the remains of the city plan *(see photo opposite page, top)* with blocks divided by parallel roads. In the surroundings, some **necropoli** have been explored as well as a sacred area including **three archaic sanctuaries**. Of great interest is the visit to the Antiquarium where the archaeological finds from the site are collected and exhibited.

In the plain to the north of the ancient city are the remains of the Doric temple known as the **"Temple of Victory"**. It was erected to commemorate the victory of the coalition of Siculo-Greek cities, led by Syracuse and Agrigento, over the Carthaginians (480 BC), marking the first Punic defeat in the Mediterranean. The temple was erected in 480-470 BC by Agrigentine craftsmen as well as by Carthaginians taken prisoner during the battle. It is a Doric hexastyle temple with 14 columns on the long sides (see attached plan), and a cell consisting of prostyle pronaos, naos and opisthodomos; also, in the ambulatory between the cell walls and the peristasis, the floor was paved with limestone slabs, a unique example among Greek temples in Sicily.

CEFALÙ

The town's ancient name, ***"Kephaloidion"***, derived from the Greek kefalè (headland, promontory), which referred to the rocky mass dominating the present-day urban area. The territory was inhabited in prehistoric times, as confirmed by the traces of human settlements found in the caves on the mountainsides. In pre-Hellenic times, the site was probably visited by the Phoenicians from the west of the island and by Greek colonists from the east, who had established trading and neighbouring relations with the population. Little is known about Cefalu's ancient history, though it probably was not a Greek colony. The most reliable historical data on the city come from Diodorus and refer to 396 BC, when the Carthaginian general Himilco entered into an alliance with its population. Later it was occupied by Dionysius, tyrant of Syracuse; in 307 BC, under the agreement with Carthage, it was conquered by Agathocles, general and tyrant of Syracuse born at Himera. In 254 BC it was conquered by the Romans following the betrayal by a faction of citizens and it enjoyed a period of prosperity, becoming a Roman "civitas decumana". In 858 AD Cefalù offered a lengthy and painful resistance to the Muslim attack. The city was burned and its population slaughtered. Under the Norman king Roger II the city entered a long period of prosperity and artistic splendour, with the foundation of the bishopric in 1131.

Right: A view of Cefalù, with the imposing Cathedral.
Top: A view of Cefalù by night, with the illuminated Cathedral.

Aerial view of the old town centre, with the monumental complex of the Cathedral and the Bishop's Palace, restored to Latin ritual in 1145 by Roger II, and the adjoining 12C cloister.
Opposite page: The Cathedral façade, flanked by the two square towers.

Bottom: A view of the time-worn cloister, surrounded by a portico with arches resting on twin columns and carved capitals. On the whole, the church is one of the most outstanding examples of 13C architecture in Sicily.

Above: Gothic window of the **"Osterio Magno"**, built in the 12C-14C, traditionally believed to be Roger II's residence in Cefalù. Situated halfway up corso Ruggero, it was linked to the coeval Osterio Piccolo, once the Ventimiglia family house, no more extant. Below, left: The medieval **public wash-house**, hewn out of the rock. Below, right: One of the picturesque alleys of the old town centre, an intricate network of typical narrow streets from the Arab and medieval period. Opposite, top: The right apse and flank of the **Cathedral**, where the original Norman structures are more evident. Bottom: A picturesque view of the façade on a plenilunary night.

The Cathedral was built by Roger II as a way of thanking the Virgin for sparing his life during a storm at sea. The king intended the church to be a "Pantheon" for the Norman dynasty. Work was started in 1131 and went on slowly under Roger's successors, William I and William II, but the original project was never completed.

The façade is preceded by the massive bell towers with four orders of single- and double-light windows, enclosing a triple-arched portico by Ambrogio da Como (1471). The magnificent portal is decorated with marble inlays of high artistic value. The right side is adorned with ogival windows and entwined blind arches. The majestic transept and apse (see photo above) are placed on a higher level than the rest of the church.

The impressive interior is basilican in plan, with a nave and two aisles divided by 16 columns with carved capitals bearing lancet arches. The church contains a fine 12C Romanesque font with four sculptured lions; the great 15C fresco depicting the Virgin and Child; two 16C statues of the Annunciation and an Angel, together with a crucifix painted on both sides, dating from the 15C and attributed to Tommaso de Vigilia. The presbytery area is considered the oldest, as confirmed by documents reporting that work on it was started on the day of Pentecost 1131.

The apse (photo above), presbytery walls and vault are entirely covered with mosaics executed by Byzantine craftsmen in 1148, as indicated by an inscription at the base of the apsidal mosaic decoration. The bowl-shaped vault (see photo, right) is dominated by the solemn figure of **"Christ Pantocrator"** giving his blessing; underneath, the Virgin Mary and four Archangels; in the lower level to the sides of the deep ogival window, the twelve Apostles. The cross vault has figures of Angels and Seraphs. In the two opposite walls of the presbytery, on four consecutive levels, there are figures of Saints and Prophets. In the middle of the left nave, a fine statue of **"Virgin and Child"** by Antonello Gagini (1533).

As shown by the photos on these pages, Cefalù, with its numerous tourist and bathing establishments, has plenty of good reasons to be a tourism-oriented town. Opposite page, top: One of the many tourist villages, camping-sites, hotels, places of amusement and typical meeting-places scattered along the coast for several kilometres, attracting tourists from all over Europe. Bottom: The gulf to the east of the urban area, with the so-called **kalura** promontory, a pleasant holiday resort with a fish-ing port and quays. Above: The small harbour. Below, left: The prehistoric sanctuary known as the **"temple of Diana"**, a megalithic structure dating from the 9C BC over which another building was erected in Greek times, turned into a church by the Byzantines. On the top of the mountain are the few remains of the **"Castle"**, one of the best fortified 13C strongholds in Sicily.

THE MANDRALISCA MUSEUM

The rooms of the Museum (Museo Comunale Mandralisca) house the archaeological and artistic collections of Baron **Enrico Piraino di Mandralisca**, including a remarkable collection of archaeological finds from the Greek, Roman and Byzantine ages. The seven rooms display painting and sculpture masterpieces, and pottery from various regions and ages: Aeolian (Bronze age), geometric (7C BC), Corinthian and Attic (6C-5C BC), as well as terracotta figures and small bronze sculptures dating from the 7C and 4C BC.

There is also a vast and remarkable collection of coins from various Siculo-Greek cities, from Lipari and Kephaloidion. The gallery includes 17C paintings of the Flemish school, a painting by **Frans Van Mieris**, Venetian views of the **Guardì** school and the famous "Portrait of an Unknown Man" by **Antonello da Messina**. The museum also contains a vast collection of minerals and shells from all over the world.

Opposite: Greek-Siceliot krater from Lipari (4C BC). The scene depicts a tunny-fish vendor arguing with the buyer.
*Above: Antonello da Messina's **"Portrait of an Unknown Man"**, painted by the great artist in 1465-70. This extraordinary work of art reveals a strong plastic realism in the face of the enigmatic smiling man.*

SEGESTA (Egesta)

The area of Segesta is one of the foremost archaeological sites in Sicily and the Mediterranean. Together with Erice and Entella, Segesta was one of the main centres founded by the Elymi, an ethnic group including immigrants from Anatolia and maybe Sican elements. The city was historically important because of its perpetual rivalry with nearby Selinunte for control over the fertile lands crossed by the Mazaro river. The earliest armed conflicts probably date back to 580-576 BC and were followed by a long succession of victories, defeats and changing alliances. In 415 BC Segesta called for Athenian help against Selinunte and Syracuse. After this disastrous expedition, it entered into an alliance with the Carthaginians which resulted in the destruction of Selinunte in 409 BC and subsequently of Himera, Agrigento and Gela.

In 397 BC Segesta, a Punic allied city, was besieged by the Syracusans and, after changing vicissitudes, at the end of the 4C BC it was conquered and destroyed by Agathocles, tyrant of Syracuse, who named the place Dikaeopolis. It was again on Carthaginian side in 306 BC, and in 267 BC it allied with Pyrrhus, King of Epirus, during his successful two-year campaign in Sicily. At the beginning of the First Punic War it was one of the first Sicilian cities to pass to the Romans, maybe because of the legendary origin shared by Trojans, Elymi and Romans. For this reason Segesta was respected by Rome and became a free and immune city; it was assigned vast territo-ries and enjoyed a period of prosperity and economic development. As its vast latifundia employed a great multitude of servants, Segesta was a starting point for the slaves' revolt led by Athenion in 104 BC. Little remarkable information exists on Roman Segesta. Excavations carried out in 1989-90 confirmed the existence of a gymnasium and the cult of the Dioscuri, and brought to light a Christian inscription dating from 524 AD. Considerable archaeological remains have been brought to light during the excavations started in 1953 by Vincenzo Tusa, including the discovery, in contrada Mango, of a temple older than the extant one on the eastern hill. This is a large temple, which probably stood in the middle of a sacred area which seems to promise further interesting discoveries.

"On the fall of Troy, some Trojans, having escaped from the Achaeans, came in boats to Sicily and settled next to the Sicans under the general name of Elymi, their cities being Erice and Segesta".

(Thucydides, book VI, 2)

THE TEMPLE OF SEGESTA

This imposing construction stands solitary and solemn in the middle of a desert landscape. The temple was probably built in the last thirty years of the 5C BC, outside the double city walls. Considered one of the most important examples of Doric style, it stands on a stepped base, covering an upper area of 61.15 x 26.25 m, over which is a peristyle with 36 unfluted columns, 6 on the fronts and 14 along the sides, still bearing the entablature and tympanums. The columns, consisting of 10-12 drums, are 9.36 m high (including the capitals), with a diameter of 1.95 m (base) and 1.56 m (top), and intercolumns of 2.40 m. The temple is crowned by the entablature and tympanums with flat metopes on the two fronts. Based on the fact that the roof is missing, many scholars have suggested that the construction of the temple was interrupted in 409 BC. Others instead believe that, since Segesta was a rich city, the roof was voluntarily left out, and the temple used as an open-air enclosure devoted to Elymian rites, with a view to bestowing nobility to it in accordance with the Doric style of Greek temples. It seems likely that, during one of the rare periods of reduced political and military tension between Segesta and Selinunte, the Segestans might have turned to the renowned workmanship of Selinuntine architects to give their main Elymian sacred building the monumental appearance of a Greek temple.

The Greek historian Thucydides thus wrote on the perpetual rivalry between the populations of Segesta and Selinunte:

"Such were the peoples, Hellenic and barbarian, inhabiting Sicily, and such was the island which the Athenians intended to invade, being ambitous in real truth of conquering the whole, although they had also the specious design of succouring their kindred and other allies in the island. They were especially incited by envoys from Segesta, who were present and invoked their aid most urgently. The Segestans had gone to war with their neighbours the Selinuntines upon questions of marriage and disputed territory, and the Selinuntines had procured the alliance of the Syracusans, and pressed Segesta hard by land and sea".

(Thucydides, book VI, 6)

*Two views of the façade of the **Doric Temple of Segesta**, still standing solitary as in the past, unspoiled by the presence of "new buildings". In front of its noble magnificence one is brought back in time and history, steeped in the beauty of a truly unique landscape.*

88

THE THEATRE OF SEGESTA

The theatre stands on the northern slopes of Monte Barbaro, on the site of the north Acropolis. Excavations carried out in 1927 under the supervision of P. Marconi have brought to light prehistoric material and remains of buildings dating from the 10C-9C BC, probably used for religious purposes, in a cave beneath the cavea.

The theatre, formerly believed to date from the mid-3C BC, actually seems to date from the second half of the 4C BC in the light of the latest archaeological research. The wide semicircular cavea, 63 m in diameter, is divided into seven wedges with twenty steps hewn out of the rock and others supported by limestone blocks. The stage is separated from the cavea by open passageways and has square parascenia decorated with two figures of the Greek divinity Pan. The theatre, which has undergone remaking and restoration work, is now used for classical drama performances every two years, thus becoming "The millenary scene for the world's classics", theatrical productions which conjure up the atmosphere of gone-by times.

As already mentioned, in contrada Mango, on a flat area beneath Monte Barbaro, recent excavations have brought to light a rectangular sanctuary surrounded by a wall of 88 x 47 m, containing the remains of a Doric temple built in two phases from the 6C to the 5C BC.

As yet no systematic research work has been carried out on the walls; only the double city walls, some gates and square towers have been found which, however, are still to be dated as regards the building and remaking stages.

Segesta's necropoli have not been located as yet and are probably still safe from despoliation by modern depredators. In recent times, excavations of the Arab and Swabian castle on the north acropolis have been started together with preliminary archaeological investigation in the urban area of ancient Segesta. In the late Roman age, part of the city was probably transferred to some other site along the road to the Segestan emporium of Castellammare, near a sulphureous water spring where remains from that age have been found. The city disappeared following the invasion by Gaiseric's Vandals, who occupied and destroyed it in c 486 AD.

Photos: The theatre overlooking the valley enclosed by Pizzo del Niviere (1042 m), where the Caldo river flows. Above and below: Remains of the Roman theatre.

CALATAFIMI - Ossuary Monument at "Pianto Romano"

"HERE WE MAKE ITALY OR DIE" Those were the words that Garibaldi addressed to Nino Bixio and to his troops on the day of the historic battle against the Bourbon army led by general Landi (15 May 1860).

On 11 May Garibaldi and his "Mille" (Thousand), supported by numerous Sicilian "picciotti" (brave fighting lads), landed at Marsala where, in the name of Italy and of Victor Emmanuel II of Savoy, he started the successful expedition which was to lead to the liberation of the whole south of Italy. On 15 May, at dawn, Garibaldi's troops arrived at Calatafimi, garrisoned by Bourbon troops. The battle broke out violently at noon and went on throughout the afternoon until, at dusk, a decisive attack by the Garibaldians put the enemy to flight. On 13 May, at Salemi, Garibaldi became dictator of Sicily in the name of Victor Emmanuel II. Triumphally welcomed by the population, the dictator continued the fight against the Bourbon army and, on 30 May, conquered Salemi thanks to the support given by the Sicilian people.

The ossuary monument is the work of the architect Ernesto Basile (1892). The bronze bas-reliefs depict some scenes from the expedition: the landing at Marsala and two episodes of the battle at Calatafimi.

*Calatafimi - **Ossuary Monument at "Pianto Romano"**. The bas-relief depicts the landing of the "Mille" at Marsala on 11 May 1860.*
*Calatafimi - **Ossuary Monument at "Pianto Romano"**. In the bas-relief, a scene from the battle won by Garibaldi's troops against the Bourbons on 15 May 1860.*

SAN VITO LO CAPO

A fishing village and now a popular seaside resort, San Vito lies along the arched sandy coastline between Capo San Vito and Punta di Solanto, at the foot of Monte Monaco. Endowed by nature with a harsh, beautiful landscape and with a clear blue sea, the town has recently witnessed a considerable urban development, encouraged by a steady flow of Italian and foreign tourists which has had a favourable impact on the local economy.

The town has a spacious fishing port equipped with docks for pleasure boats, and high-level accomodation facilities including camping-sites and tourist villages. In some caves at Piana di Sopra, engravings from the Upper Paleolithic have been found, depicting deer, anthropomorphous and linear figures.

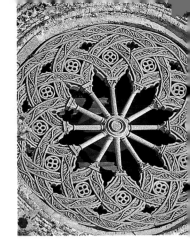

ERICE

A naturally fortified Elymian city, Erice had one of the most famous pagan sanctuaries, dedicated to the goddess of fertility called Astarte by the Phoenicians, Aphrodite by the Greeks and Venus Erycina by the Romans. The goddess was the protector of sailors, venerated by all Mediterranean peoples, and the sacred site was regularly attended by pilgrims and believers. In Roman times, even though it had lost its importance as a fortified site, the sanctuary was put at the head of a religious confederation including 17 Sicilian cities, and protected by a Roman garrison. Under Tiberius, the whole sacred area was restored, thus maintaining its original religious importance. The city became a Carthaginian stronghold and was stormed by Pyrrhus in 277 BC and reconquered by the Carthaginians in 275 BC. During the First Punic War it was destroyed by the Carthaginian army in 260 BC, with the subsequent deportation of its inhabitants to Drepano, present-day Trapani. No remarkable historical information exists on Byzantine Erice; the town was still inhabited and its fertile surroundings were scattered with farms. Towards 831 AD the stronghold was occupied by the Arabs and called Gebel-Hamed. Under the Normans, in the 12C, a period of great prosperity began; the town was repopulated and underwent radical transformations which gave it its present-day peculiar appearance.

*Photos: The exterior of the **Church of the Assunta**, preceded by the massive chiaramontano bell tower. Top, left: One of the double-light windows of the bell tower. Right: The recently redone rose window, an accurate reproduction of the original one.*

Opposite page: Some details of the interior, rebuilt in neo-Gothic style in the 19C, with the columns and arches of the original construction.

ERICE - Chiesa Matrice or Church of the Assunta

It was built in 1314 by Frederick of Aragon, who had taken up residence in the city, shortly after the anti-French popular uprising known as the Sicilian Vespers. The façade of the church maintains its original Gothic style, while the portico with pointed arches dates from the 15C. The detached bell tower was originally a watch-tower, built a few years earlier. The 13C interior was completely transformed by the lengthy and complex rebuilding work started in 1865, so that only the two-aisled plan and the two rows of columns bearing pointed arches remain of the original structure. In the side chapels, two statues of **"Madonna with Child"** (one from **Laurana's** school) and a Madonna attributed to Domenico Gagini. An imposing marble statue by Giuliano Mancino, dating from 1523, stands out in the presbytery; the Crucifix chapel has a 15C Gothic-Catalan star-shaped vault.

In the photos, a survey of Erice's history through the centuries. Top, left: The interior of the so-called **"Castle of Venus"**, the site of the famous sanctuary of **"Venus Erycina"** and of the superimposed Norman stronghold built in the 12C-13C. Top: The exterior of the stronghold and the imposing structure of the governor's castle redone during the last century. Middle: Two views of the **ancient Punic walls** with the arches opened by the Normans. The huge megalithic blocks dating from the 7C-6C BC and restructured in Roman times can still be seen in the lower part of the walls, while the upper parts date from the Norman and Aragonese periods. Under the Normans the name of the city was changed into Monte San Giuliano by Roger, who had had a vision of the saint during the siege of the Arab stronghold.

Bottom, left: The **"Torretta Pepoli"**, a 17C construction built for Count Agostino Pepoli, the Trapanese patron responsible for the restoration of the **"Balio"** (the crenellated castle with fortified towers) and the English-style garden with a magnificent view of the Val d'Erice and the plain of Bonagia. See photo below. Left: The remains of the so-called **"Spanish quarters"**, Spanish barracks dating from the early 17C. In the background the cone-shaped top of Monte Cofano (659 m), Monte Monaco and Capo San Vito with the vast and fertile plain of Bonagia, housing an old 16C "tonnara" (tunny-fishery).

SCOPELLO

An old agricultural village, Scopello stretches to the sides of an 18C "baglio" (here, a sort of large manor house with buildings opening onto a central courtyard), on the site of a pre-existing Arab hamlet. In the photo, the beautiful small cove with the 16C buildings of the "tonnara" (tunnyfishery), established in the 12C and active until a few years ago. The charm of its rocky coastline and the beauty of the landscape make it one of the most emblematic and extraordinary places in the island. Within a short distance, on the slopes of Monte Speziale, in the coastal area between Scopello and San Vito Lo Capo, there is the "Zingaro Regional Natural Reserve". This is an untouched oasis of Mediterranean vegetation, with carrob trees, dwarf palms of exceptional size, wildolives, the typical Mediterranean maquis with brooms, asphodels, euphorbias and, in the early Sicilian spring, luxuriant irises, gillyflowers, daffodils and calendulas. Looking west, towards San Vito Lo Capo, a foot-path on the slopes of the mountains winds its way across the natural reserve, in a beautiful coastal landscape dominated by 16C watch-towers.

CASTELLAMMARE DEL GOLFO

In pre-Hellenic times, the town on the gulf was used as a landing place and trade emporium by the Elymian populations of Erice and Segesta. In the early Middle Ages, it was fortified so as to protect the port, where the loading of wheat and other agricultural products was carried out. The original castle, probably built in Arab times, was restructured with a view to establishing a tunny-fishery. The stronghold was rebuilt in Norman-Swabian times and strengthened in the 14C by the Aragonese, who isolated it by cutting an isthmus. After the construction of a new outer breakwater, the port continued to handle trade exchanges, and to be a landing place for fishing and pleasure boats. In the old town centre, facing via Garibaldi, there is the *chiesa Madre*, the main church, built in the 17C and restructured several times in the course of the following centuries. In via Ponte Castello is the *chiesetta del Rosario*, a small church with a rich 16C portal. Further on is the promontory dominated by the *"Castle"* to the right of the port with the quay where small fishing boats are tied up.
At the bottom, the promontory with the Castle (right) and a view of the town (left).

EGADI ISLANDS

The Egadi islands, the ancient Aegates, are ***Favignana***, the main island and municipal centre, ***Levanzo***, ***Marettimo***, and the islets of ***Formica***, the site of an abandoned tunny-fishery, and ***Maraone***. Situated within a short distance from Trapani (Marettimo, the furthest, is only 38 km off the coast), they have been inhabited since prehistoric times (Upper Paleolithic), as witnessed by the finds made in the caves of Favignana and Levanzo.

In **Favignana** (right, top), the ancient Aegusa, the presence of a Phoenician-Punic settlement was revealed by a Punic inscription on the wall of a hypogeum. Carthaginian naval bases during the Punic Wars, the islands were occupied by the Romans in 241 BC following the victory of Consul Lutatius Catulus over the Carthaginian fleet in the waters off Favignana. In Norman times, the San Giacomo Fort and the Santa Caterina Fort were built to defend the main island. Favignana is the seat of the most important tunny-fishery in Sicily, where the traditional "mattanza" (tunny killing) takes place every year. Fishing is still the main economic activity, together with tourism in the summer months.

Levanzo, the ancient Phorbantia, is geologically and prehistorically important because of its caves, in which finds from the Upper Paleolithic have been brought to light. Inside the Grotta del Genovese (Genoese cave), rock drawings and paintings have been discovered which, according to experts, testify to cultural "facies" from different ages (Paleolithic-Mesolithic). Two series of drawings decorate the walls: one with animal figures (cattle, horses, deer), the other with human figures hunting or dancing and idols suggesting the performance of propitiatory rites. A pleasant boat trip can be taken along the steep coasts of the island, scattered with grottoes opening out on to the sea and dominated by the ***Faraglione***, a cone-shaped rock connected to the land by a short isthmus.

Marettimo, anciently called Hiera or Hieromesus (see photo above), is mostly mountainous except for the short stretch of coast along which the urban area and the small harbour lie. From its highest point, Monte Falcone (686 m), there is a sweeping view of the entire island and the nearby coast of Trapani. With its springs and its clear and unspoiled sea swarming with fish, Marettimo is the most fascinating of the Egadi islands. By taking a boat trip along its coasts, one can fully appreciate the natural and geological richness of this island, scattered with marine grottoes, small coves and picturesque rocks all along its steep cliffs.

TRAPANI

The primitive settlement on the site of present-day Trapani developed around the village of Drepano or Drapano. The Greeks called it Drepanon (sickle), possibly because of the sickle-shaped stretch of land on which the original nucleus of the city formed, and the name was later maintained by the Romans (Drepanum). Because of its strategic position along the Mediterranean trade routes, in the 8C BC it became a Phoenician emporium and then a Punic city, one of the foremost Carthaginian naval bases, together with Lilybaeum, Motya and Panormo, in the framework of the Punic strategic apparatus in western Sicily. The surroundings of Trapani, including the Egadi islands, are scattered with evidence of human settlements dating from the Paleolithic. The traces of the Homo Sapiens are more evident in the coastal caves, but most of all in the Grotta del Genovese on the island of Levanzo. There, drawn on the cave walls, prehistoric man left to posterity an enduring record of his daily life, hunting habits, rites, and natural surroundings.

According to ancient sources, Drepanon served as a port and trading base for the population of Erice. In 260 BC, during the First Punic War, the Carthaginian Hamilcar Barca destroyed Erice, transferring its inhabitants to Drepanon and fortifying the city with new walls and watch-towers.

In the summer of 249 BC, the Romans were defeated by Adherbal's Carthaginian fleet in the waters off Drepanon. Eight years later, in 241 BC, the Carthaginians were finally defeated by the fleet of Consul Lutatius Catulus in the decisive naval battle of the Egadi islands. Drepanum passed under Roman rule and a slow decline began for the city. As the Censor's seat, it was affected by a profound crisis, which was reflected in the urban layout, as witnessed by the scarce archaeological finds from the Roman age. The city's destiny improved in the course of the following centuries. In the 9C, it was conquered by the Arabs and, under the Normans in 1077, it was elevated to the rank of a privileged royal city and enjoyed a period of trading and maritime economic prosperity which lasted throughout the following centuries under the Aragonese. The latter reclaimed the neighbouring regions and extended the urban area by adding new quarters, building the Castle, opening new roads and urbanizing the coastal areas, a process which continued under Charles V in the 16C.

*Photo: Panorama of **Trapani**, with the quarters from different epochs, ranging from the Muslim age to the 17C, and the post-war building interventions following the extensive bombings of the city. Boats link the city to the **Egadi** islands and North Africa, establishing trade relations with Italian and European ports. On the following pages: a view of the Trapanese "saline" (salt-pans) at sunset.*

PALAZZO DELLA GIUDECCA

Situated in the old city centre, in via della Giudecca, the heart of the old Jewish quarter, this Catalan-styled building is flanked by a tower which is entirely covered by diamond-pointed ashlars in the upper side, as is the ogival portal with richly ornate windows. In the courtyard the older remains of the construction are still visible.

THE ANNUNZIATA SANCTUARY

The main body of this building, which was erected between 1315 and 1332, was entirely rebuilt in 1760. Of the original structure, the façade with a rose window and the 15C Gothic portal still remain. The fine Baroque bell tower, with pilaster strips and half-columns, dates from 1650. The single-naved interior was restructured in the 18C by Giovanni B. Amico and contains remarkable works of art: a **Virgin and Child** by Nino

Pisano, known as the "Madonna di Trapani"; the **"Fishermen's Chapel"**, used as a baptistery since 1468, with a groin vault frescoed in the 16C with a story from the Genesis; the 16C **"Sailors' Chapel"** in Renaissance style with Gothic and Arab-Norman reminescences. In the Sanctuary or the Virgin's Chapel, which is reached through a bronze gate designed by Giuliano Musarra (1591), there is a magnificent marble arch with relief figures of Prophets and the Eternal Father, the work of Antonio and Giacomo Gagini. On the polychrome marble altar of St Albert's Chapel is the silver statue of the saint by Vincenzo Bonaiuto.

The **Pepoli Regional Museum** (Museo Regionale Pepoli) displays interesting collections of archaeological finds, paintings, sculptures and other artistic items. Particularly noteworthy is the collection of items by **Trapanese coral craftsmen**, masters of an art which has developed here since the second half of the 16C. Today a new school, following in the footsteps of the ancient tradition, is giving fresh impetus to this precious and creative handicraft activity.

The **"salt road"** offers another interesting itinerary through the salt-pans and pools all along the coast between Trapani and Marsala, with a visit to the **"Salt Museum"** (Museo del Sale) at Nubia.

Top, left: A sight of the sea-front buildings, with a view of the Cathedral dome from the port in which small fishing and pleasure boats berth. Bottom: View of the city from the panoramic road leading to Erice, with the Egadi islands. Above: The neo-Gothic palace housing the Banco di Sicilia, which still has a 16C arched portal with ashlars.

The best clue to understanding Trapani is undoubtedly the sea. Ever since the 8C BC, the sea has been a mainstay of the city's economy. Fishing, the main sector, has always been accompanied by other sea-related activities including coral fishing, salt extraction in the long-established salt-pans, and maritime trade. It would be interesting to just walk about the historic quarters which have characterized the life and culture of ancient Trapani, where the architectural stratifications of the urban layout are still evident.

*Above: The **Ligny Tower**, erected in 1671 by the Viceroy Claudio Lamoraldo, Prince of Ligny. The building, originally a watch-tower, now houses the History and Prehistory Museum. Below: One of the windmills which characterize the Trapanese seascape, now restored as a vestige of the past. Opposite, top: The stretch of water of the outer port, protected by the **Colombaia islands**, with the 14C octagonal tower and the 15C fortress. Opposite, bottom: A spectacular view of the Trapanese **salt-pans** during salt extraction and piling up.*

MOZIA

The **Stagnone** lagoon is one of the most fascinating landscapes in Sicily. Several small islands covered with Mediterranean maquis enclose a vast stretch of water, protected from the open sea by the low contours of Isola Lunga. A natural haven for sailors, with waters swarming with fish: in the 8C BC, it must have appeared to the Phoenicians as the ideal place to establish the first base of their trade empire in the western Mediterranean. As the power of Carthage grew, Motya became the main Punic military base, continuously at war with the Siculo-Greek cities. In 397 BC it was conquered and destroyed by Dionysius I of Syracuse. It was reconquered by the Carthaginians the following year, and a new community was founded at Lilybaeum. This event marked Motya's destiny, as the city, inhabited until the 3C BC, never recovered and eventually vanished from history.

The island is entirely covered with the remains of the ancient city, surrounded by a long stretch of walls with watch-towers, two main gates and several smaller ones scattered along a perimeter of about 3 km. The North Gate opens on to a road which used to join the island to Birgi, on the mainland; in ancient times the road, now submerged, was 1 m above the Stagnone waters. It would be interesting to visit the ***archaic necropolis*** (late 8C-6C BC), consisting of cinerary tombs cut out of the rock. Not far away is the ***"tophet"***, a Phoenician sanctuary where first-born children were sacrificed to Baal Hammon. The discovery of ancient Motya was made possible by the enthusiastic work of the English merchant Giuseppe Whitaker, the owner of the island, who directed the first successful excavations during the last century. Mozia's Museum displays the archaeological material found on the island, in the Birgi necropolis and in ancient Lilybaeum. The most interesting item is a beautiful ***marble statue*** found in 1979 in Motya and portraying a young man dressed in a long pleated tunic enhancing his strong athletic figure, the work of a Greek artist from the 5C BC.

Above: An emblematic aerial view of the Stagnone lagoon. In the foreground, the geometrically arranged salt-pans and the sea-linked canals. In the middle, the island on which the ancient Phoenician-Punic city of Motya is located; in the background, towards the open sea, the stretch of land of Isola Lunga.

Above: The **"cothon"**, a sort of basin which an artificial canal joined to the sea. It was probably used as a dry dock or as a cultural site where religious rites were performed. It is surrounded by a wall and paved with tuff ashlars. On the lower side of the canal are the remains of small barracks.

Below: A stretch of coast with boundary walls and the foundations of the urban buildings of ancient Motya. This was the north side of the city, where the main public buildings, places of worship and temples, probably dedicated to the Phoenician goddess Astarte, once stood.

Above: A panoramic aerial view of the present-day town; its wide harbour handles cargo ships over 5,000 tons used for wine export.
Below: The stele erected on the rocky Capo Boeo marks the westernmost point of Sicily; from the sea round terrace there is a sweeping view of the Egadi islands, the Stagnone, Mozia and Monte Erice.

MARSALA

The Punic name **Lilybaeum**, from Capo Boeo, was changed by the Arabs into Marsa-Alì or Allah, hence Marsala. According to ancient sources, the origins of the city are linked to the destruction of Motya (a Phoenician city founded in the 8C BC) by Dionysius I tyrant of Syracuse, in 397 BC. Refugees from Motya fled to Capo Boeo and, perhaps together with native populations, founded the city of Lilybaeum. In 350 BC the city was fortified and became one of the Carthaginian strongholds in Sicily. Conquered by the Romans in 241 BC, it maintained its military and commercial power in the central Mediterranean and became the quaestor's seat for the western provinces.

Under the Arabs, who conquered it in 830 AD, the city continued to flourish as a hub of trade with the African continent. The Normans conquered Marsala in 1072. Between the 12C and 14C, the medieval urban layout was developed, with the construction of religious buildings and monasteries. The city took on its present Renaissance-Baroque aspect between the 17C and 18C, when the main civil and religious buildings were erected or reconstructed and surrounded by a circle of squared bastions with four monumental gateways. Today the city's economy is mostly based on wine industry, particularly on the production of the famous Marsala wine, introduced by the Englishman G. Woodhouse in 1773 and continued by the Ingham and Florio families with the establishment of new and modern wineries throughout the region.

Opposite page, top: **Porta Garibaldi** (formerly Porta di Mare), built in 1685 and renamed in memory of the landing of Garibaldi's troops on 11 May 1860.
Bottom, left: The Baroque façade of the **chiesa del Collegio dei Gesuiti**, a church built in 1589-1592. Right: The **Cathedral** (Duomo), dedicated to St Thomas of Canterbury, built in 1628 over a pre-existing Norman construction; the interior is richly decorated with notable works of art.

SELINUNTE

The monumental ruins of the ancient Greek city of Selinunte stretch over a plateau facing the African sea and over the gentle hills surrounding it. This is one of the most notable archaeological sites in the Mediterranean, if not the foremost, in that it testifies to the architectural evolution of Doric temple art in Sicily.

The majestic and outstanding ruins of the temples, the remains of the powerful walls and fortifications, the urban layout, the necropoli, offer a unique and unrivalled view of a 5C BC Greek city on the island, conveying information on both the city plan and the structural and artistic conception of temples with the variations in style which have occurred in the course of the centuries.

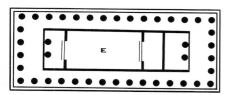

In the photos, two views of **temple E**, probably dedicated to **Hera**, the Roman Juno, as confirmed by a votive stele found in the temple, with a dedicatory inscription to the goddess. The edifice measures 70.20 x 27.05 m. Re-erected in the mid-1950s, it is one of the most significant examples of pure Doric style.

Ancient historical sources are controversial as to the date of Selinunte's foundation. According to Diodorus, the city was founded between 651 and 650 BC, while according to Thucydides its foundation dates from 629-628 BC. The Athenian historian thus reports:"...*Here they (the inhabitants of the Hyblaean Megara) lived two hundred and forty-five years, after which they were expelled from the city and the country by Gelon, tyrant of Syracuse. Before their expulsion, however, a hundred years after they had founded Megara, they sent out Pamillus and founded Selinunte; he having come from their mother country Megara to join them in its foundation*". The first urban nucleus was established on the vast sheer plateau (about 50 m above sea level) situated between the valley of the Modione river (the ancient Selinos) to the west, and the "Gorgo di Cottone" valley to the east. This was the Acropolis, of which the Temples A, B, C, D and O remain; behind it, to the north, were the city residential quarters. The name Selinunte probably derived from the river which flew to the west of the city boundaries, the Selinos, or, as others have suggested, from a wild plant, a kind of celery ("selinon"), which still grows locally and whose leaves were depicted on the early coins minted at Selinunte. The westernmost Greek outpost, closely in contact with the Carthaginian-Punic territories and with the Elymian cities of Segesta and Entella, the city extended its influence over the fertile coastal plains, from the mouth of the Platani river to the east, to the mouth

Right: The bronze statue known as "The Ephebus of Selinunte", found in 1882, a Greek work of art characterized by an indigenous "facies", dating from the 5C BC.

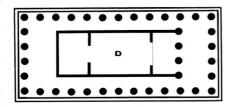

The ruins of **temple D** in the acropolis, with the flight of steps and several drums of the columns of the east front. The deity to whom the temple was dedicated is still uncertain. Researchers have suggested Jupiter Agoraeus or Aphrodite, the goddess of love.

of the Mazarus river to the west, as far as present-day Poggioreale (destroyed and evacuated following a violent earthquake in the 1980s) to the north, behind the Elymian city of Entella. In the late 6C BC Selinunte had to fight against the Elymian coalition of Erice, Segesta and Alicyae. These early skirmishes and territorial controversies were followed by a long period of peaceful neighbouring relations, which was accompanied by the urban and architectural development of the city: the majestic temples were built and the Acropolis was surrounded by powerful fortifications; docks and emporiums were created to support maritime trade.

Farmlands were extensively cultivated, trade with the other Greek colonies of Sicily, with the cities of Magna Graecia and the Etruscans was intensified and Selinunte's ships reached as far as the North-African coasts. As Diodorus wrote in his "Histories", Selinunte was the only Greek colony to be aligned with Carthage during the first Punic invasion of Sicily, ending in 480 BC with the Carthaginian defeat at Himera. Selinunte

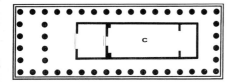

Temple C. A Doric peripteral hexastyle temple dating from to the first half of the 6C BC. It has been defined archaic for the length of its plan and for the presence of monolithic columns. In the interior, the cella consisted of a pronaos, naos and adyton and the front had two rows of six columns each.

was not subjected to retaliation by the Greeks (Syracusans and Agrigentines) leading the successful coalition. In the 6C BC the Selinuntines founded a sub-colony, which they called **Heraclea Minoa**, on the plateau dominating the Halikos, the present-day Platani river. In the fifth book of his "History", Herodotus wrote: *"Other Spartans accompanied Dorieus on his voyage as co-founders, namely Thessalus, Paraebates, Celeas, and Euryleon. These men and all their troops reached Sicily, but there they fell in a battle wherein they were defeated by the Segestans and Phoenicians, only one of the founders, Euryleon, surviving the disaster. He then, collecting the remnants of the army, made himself master of Minoa, the Selinuntine colony, and helped the Selinuntines to throw off the yoke of their tyrant Pythagoras. Having defeated Pythagoras, he sought to become tyrant in his room, and he even reigned at Selinunte for a short time, but after a while the Selinuntines rose up in revolt against him, and though he fled to the altar of Jupiter Agoraeus, they notwithstanding put him to death".*

After the defeat at Himera, Selinunte changed its policy and allied with Syracuse until its fall in 409 BC, when Carthage, eager for revenge, besieged the city with its powerful and warlike army led by Hannibal, son of Gisco. After a vain resistance, the city was conquered and destroyed. A cruel massacre followed, causing the death of sixteen thousand and the capture of five thousand inhabitants. Hannibal ended the siege by demolishing the city walls and temples. It was during the First Punic War that Selinunte's power and prestige were finally given the coup de grace. In order to prevent it from falling in Roman hands, the Carthaginians dismantled all the residual fortifications and destroyed the inhabited areas, transferring the population to Lilybaeum. This dramatic event, in 250 BC, marked the end of Selinunte's power and the abandonment of the city. The Roman age did not witness any particular recovery of the city life. In Byzantine times, a catastrophic earthquake dealt a deathblow to the remnants of the city, and magnificent Selinunte was forever swept away from history.

A fine view of the site of ancient Selinunte as seen from above.

THE DEMETER MALOPHOROS SANCTUARY

Opposite, two views of the **Malophoros** sacred area, situated to the west of the Modione river, the ancient **Selinos**. Top, the ruins of the propylaeum which gave access to the **temenos of Demeter**, leading to the goddess' sacred enclosure through the sacred path. Demeter was the daughter of Kronos and Rhea, hence sister of Zeus, and mother of Persephone, born from an incestous relationship with Zeus. Hesiod handed down this Olympian episode in his Theogony: *"Then he (Zeus) came to the bed of all-nourishing Demeter, and she bore white-armed Persephone, whom Hades carried off from her mother"*.

Demeter was the goddess of vegetation, fields and agriculture, so no wonder that the colonists, who had settled there attracted by the fertility of the soil, built this sanctuary in her honour. Bottom, a view of the **temenos of Demeter Malaphoros**, erected in the style of the earliest temples, recalling the pre-Doric **"megaron"**. On the same site, another sacred enclosure dedicated to **Zeus Melichios** and one dedicated to **Pasicratea**, the name given by the inhabitants of Selinunte to Persephone or Kore, the daughter of Demeter, wife of Pluto and thus lady of the underworld and of the dead. Another enclosure to the left of the propylaeum was dedicated to **Hecate** or **Artemis triform**, a three-faced deity: **Hecate**, **Artemis and Proserpina**, represented by a single body with lion, horse and she-wolf heads. Outside the Malophoros enclosure, archaeological excavations have brought to light a construction dating from the 6C BC, referred to as **Temple M**, measuring 20.40 x 10.85 m and recently identified as a monumental fountain with access from a flight of steps.

THE ROCCA DI CUSA QUARRIES

The modelled limestone blocks are scattered all over the ground, as if they had just been extracted from the rock. The landscape is characterized by the rural environment typical of this part of Sicily, abounding in vines, olives, almond and fig trees, secluded as it certainly must have been 2300 years ago, when Selinuntine quarrymen extracted the cylindrical blocks used to make columns for their temples. It is the sad, silent image of one day in Selinunte, when the omnipresent Carthaginian menace descended on the city, bringing forth death and destruction. Looking around, it seems as if the quarrymen's work should be resumed before long. But this will no longer happen: we are in the year 409 BC, the very day when the terrible historic events began which would eventually lead to the annihilation of their city; the work of the Selinuntine masters has forever stopped, never to be resumed again.

SCIACCA (Monte Kronio)

Identified as the ancient ***Termae Selinuntinae***, the modern town lies on a long stretch of terraced hillside dominating the wide fishing port. For the abundance of thermal waters on the slopes of Monte San Calogero, a 360 m high calcareous mountain dominating the town, Sciacca is the first spa town in Sicily, known since ancient times for the therapeutic properties of its waters and natural "stufe vaporose", hot caves full of dense steam coming out from the karst cavities on the top of the mountain. According to Diodorus, the first to exploit the town's hydrothermal basin was Daedalus. The territory has been inhabited since the Neolithic and Aeneolithic Ages (5000-3000 BC), as witnessed by the important prehistoric remains found in the caves. The old town centre offers an interesting itinerary, among monuments ranging from the Middle Ages to the 17C and the Baroque 18C.

HERACLEA MINOA

The city, situated on a plateau gently sloping to the sea near the mouth of the Platani river, was founded by the Selinuntines in the 6C BC, presumably on the site of a Mycenaean commercial settlement. The name Heraclea was added by the Spartan Euryleon, the head of a group of new colonists who settled in the city after taking part in Dorieus' unsuccessful campaign in Sicily. The name Minoa is related to Minos, the legendary Cretan king who, having come to Sicily on an expedition, was killed in the royal palace of the Sican king Kokalos.

The foundation of Minoa by the Selinuntines was part of their plans to expand their city eastwards, in competition with Agrigento. In the early 5C BC, Minoa passed to Theron, tyrant of Agrigento (488-472 BC) who, having identified the site of Minos' tomb, returned his bones to the Cretans, as reported by the Siculo-Greek historian Diodorus in the fourth book of his Histories. Involved in the Greek-Carthaginian wars, the city was destroyed and sacked.

Under the Romans it became a "civitas decumana", as Cicero reported in his *Verrines*. It was abandoned at the end of the 1C AD and eventually disappeared from history.

AGRIGENTO

The Agrigento area was inhabited since prehistoric times, as witnessed by archaeological finds dating from the Copper and Bronze Ages. The Aeneolithic settlement of **Serraferlicchio** has made it possible to identify and date a particular indigenous "facies" of prehistoric Sicily through the discovery of a large quantity of well-made pottery with black decorations on a red background. The earliest traces of Greek presence date back to the end of the 7C BC, as witnessed by the **archaic necropolis of Montelusa**, situated on the coast to the west of present-day San Leone, Agrigento's seaside residential quarter, near the confluence of the rivers Hipsas and Akragas (now Sant'Anna and San Biagio) which, before flowing into the sea, join into a single river, the San Leone, whence the site name. According to Thucydides, Akragas was founded in 580 BC: "about one hundred and eight years after the foundation of Gela, the Geloans founded Akragas, so called from the river bearing that name, and named **Aristonous** and **Pystilus** their founders, giving their own institutions to the colony" (Thucydides, book VI, 4). The foundation of the city marked an important step in the plan by the Rhodian-Cretans from Gela to expand their political and military influence towards the northern coasts and the hinterland.

*Photos: Two views of the so-called temple of the **Dioscuri**. The name derives from the Greek **"Dios kuroi"**, i.e. "**Sons of Zeus**", the twins Castor and Pollux who, according to Spartan primitive mythology, emerged with Helen and Clytemnestra from the egg conceived by Leda with Zeus, who appeared to her in the form of a swan. The four extant columns were re-erected in the course of the last century. A Doric peripteral hexastyle temple, it is 38.69 x 16.63 m in size, with 13 columns on the longer sides.*

THE VALLEY OF THE TEMPLES

Top: The majestic ruins of the temple dedicated to **Olympian Zeus**. Steps lead up to the sacrificial altar, preceding the east front of the gigantic **Olympieion**. The temple, based on a very ingenious and innovative design, was built after the Agrigentine and Syracusan victory over the Carthaginians at Himera in 480 BC. Punic prisoners taken during the successful battle were employed for its construction, and it was still un-finished when, in 406 BC, the city was conquered and burnt during the Carthaginian retaliatory attack. For its majestic proportions, it is considered to be the largest temple in the western world together with **temple G** at Selinunte. Its structure did not comply with traditional Doric schemes: on the rectangular base (56.30 x 113.45 m) were five steps leading to the perimetrical ambulatories; it was a pseudo-peripteral temple, surrounded by a wall out of which jutted 7 x 14 half-columns, each corresponding to an internal pillar; in the middle of the wide intercolumns, at about 13 m from the stylobate, were the plastic figures of gigantic **"telamones"** which decorated the exterior and which contributed, together with the pillars and half-columns, in supporting the heavy entablature (see photo opposite).

THE TEMPLE OF CONCORD is one of the best preserved Doric temples of the ancient Greek world, with the **Temple of Hera and Paestum** (Posidonion) and the Athenian **Theseion**. Its perfect state of conservation is due to the fact that it has continued to be used in the course of

The ancient history of Agrigento is mainly linked to the figure of Phalaris, described as a cruel tyrant to whom, on the other hand, the city owed its early, rapid development: the area, protected to the north by the hill which constituted the Acropolis, the **Rupe Atenea**, extended as far as the valley dominated by the low hill on which the monumental Doric temples were built. During Phalaris' rule, from 570 to 555 BC, Akragas grew more powerful and extended its possessions to the detriment of the Sicans, who were driven back towards the hinterland or subdued. The expansionist policy was continued by Phalaris' successor, the tyrant Theron (488-472 BC), who brought the city to the height of its splendour. After the victory at Himera in 480 BC over the Carthaginians, he pushed the city boundaries as far as the Tyrrhenian coasts and the coastline between the mouth of the Salso, the southern Himera, and that of the Halikos, the present-day Platani, to the south. This first armed clash was followed by a prosperous and active period, marked by the construction of temples, public and private buildings and fortifications. At that time, Agrigento probably had the highest standard of living among all the Greek cities in Sicily, as witnessed by Empedocles, a physician, thaumaturge, philosopher and orator, the city's most distinguished citizen of all times, renowned also in Greece, who thus defined his fellow citizens: "The Agrigentines enjoy the pleasures and luxuries of this world as if they were to die the next day, but make their buildings as if they were to live forever". And we can well believe him, if a coeval Agrigentine physician, a certain Acron, given his patients' methodical pursue of epicurean excess, felt the need to exhort his fellow citizens to be moderate in a book entitled "The Healthy People's Diet". Thus Pindar, the Greek lyric poet who lived between 518 and 438 BC, sang the praises of Agrigento: "Thee I invoke, city of Persephone, the most beautiful city of mortal men, lover of splendour rising by Akragas over the towered hill..." (Pindar, *12th Pythian Ode*). Apart from luxury and opulence, Theron's court promoted poetry and art and attracted scientists, philosophers, sculptors and painters such as Pythagoras, Myron, Simonides and Zeuxis. The Agrigentines normally practised sports, particularly equestrian sports, and there were horsemen and charioteers among them who had scored more than one victory at Olympia.

Towards the mid-5C BC, a democratic regime was established and for some years, following the victory at Himera, the city enjoyed a period of relative peace until the Carthaginian return to Sicily. In 406 BC Agrigento was besieged and burnt by the Carthaginian general Himilco, and its population sought refuge in Leontinoi, under Syracusan protection. Under Timoleon, who defeated the Carthaginians (c 340 BC) and is considered Agrigento's second founder, the city arose again from its ruins and was given a new urban layout, as witnessed by the remains of the Hellenistic-Roman quarter.

*time; in 597 AD, it was transformed into a Christian basilica by the Agrigentine Bishop Gregory. A peripteral hexastyle temple with 6 x 13 columns, it rises in the middle of the Hill of the Temples, dominating with its elegant proportions the valleys of the ancient urban centre to the north and the valley sloping towards the African sea to the south, as it was seen by the Latin poet Virgil who described it in the Aeneid: "Then Akragas, with lofty summits crown'd, long for the race of warlike steeds renown'd" (transl. by J. Dryden, The Harvard Classics). Following pages: The **Temple of Concord** displays its perfect architectural structure, in the purest Doric style.*

THE TEMPLE OF HERA LACINIA

The name of the temple is due to confusion with the temple of Hera at Crotone, on the Lacinio promontory, of which only a column from the east side remains. Hera was the daughter of Kronos and Rhea, sister and wife of Zeus and the mother of all the Olympian gods. She hated Hector and the Trojans and persecuted them incessantly, until Zeus promised their fusion with the Latins to create a new people. The great Roman poet Virgil thus wrote in the Aeneid: "From blood so mixed, a pious race shall flow,/ Equal to gods, excelling all below./ No nation more respect to you shall pay,/ Or greater off'rings on your altars lay". (Virgil, *Aeneid* XII, 419, transl. by J. Dryden, The Harvard Classics). The Romans identified the Greek goddess with Juno, sister and wife of Jupiter, lunar celestial goddess of women, fertility, marriage and fidelity.

The temple stands on the highest point of the **Hill of the Temples**, on a beautiful panoramic site. Built in the purest Doric style on a four-stepped stylobate, it is 38.15 x 16.90 m in size, with 34 columns, 6 on the fronts and 13 on the long sides.

It is a peripteral hexastyle temple with an in-antis cella (28.68 x 9.93 m); part of the boundary walls and several drums of the columns of the opisthodomos and pronaos are still visible.

It was built shortly before the Temple of Concord, dating from the second half of the 5C BC, with obvious architectural similarities. Burnt by the Carthaginians in 406 BC, it was restored by the Romans. Near the east front is a large **sacrificial altar** (29.80 x 7.25 m); opposite, there was the opening of Gate III, with the fortifications and the access road with the tracks left by carts.

The so-called **"mule of Dionysos"**, from the chthonic deities area (c 500 BC). The mule is carrying a kàntharos for the transport of wine on his back.

The marble torso of a **Greek warrior**, whose fragments were found in 1940 among the layers of ruins around the **Temple of Zeus**. The warrior, fallen on his knees, defends himself from behind a shield. The statue (480-475 BC) was reconstructed by Prof. De Miro, who has suggested that this masterpiece of figurative art might be the work of an eminent artist, **Pythagoras of Rhegium**.

THE REGIONAL ARCHAEOLOGICAL MUSEUM

The Museum (Museo Archeologico Regionale), established in the monumental area of the **bouleuterion** and **ekklesi-asterion**, on the hillock of San Nicola, and incorporating part of the convent adjoining the church of the same name, is one of the foremost archaeological museums in Sicily. The material is arranged chronologically and divided into two main sectors, one concerning Agrigento and its territory and the other concerning part of the archaeological sites of the provinces of Caltanissetta and Gela, which have their own museums. **Room 1** houses maps and plans of Agrigento and the Museum plan. **Room 2**, pre-proto-historic material dating from the 2nd and 1st millennia BC and relating to the native populations and the area on which the Greek **Akragas** was founded by the Rhodio-Cretans (580 BC); material from the necropoli, chronologically arranged in showcases; Early and Medium Bronze Age pottery from the **Aeneololithic culture of Serraferlicchio**, from Cannatello and Monserrato, and Early Iron Age material from **the culture of S. Angelo Muxaro**.

Room 3 displays the collection of vases pertaining to the civic museum and the Giudice collection, including items from the latest excavations. The rigorously chronological itinerary includes **red-figured and black-figured Attic vases** dating from the 6C and 5C BC and the Graeco-Italiot production from the 5C-3C BC. The 19 rooms of the Museum preserve the invaluable historical and artistic vestiges of the Greek Akragas and of the area under its dominion.

A small Mycenaean amphora from the marina of **Girgenti** (Agrigento's Arabic name), dating from the 14C BC and bearing witness to the contacts between the Greek world and **Sicania** recorded by literary tradition. Below: An outstanding vase from the Museum's valuable collection.

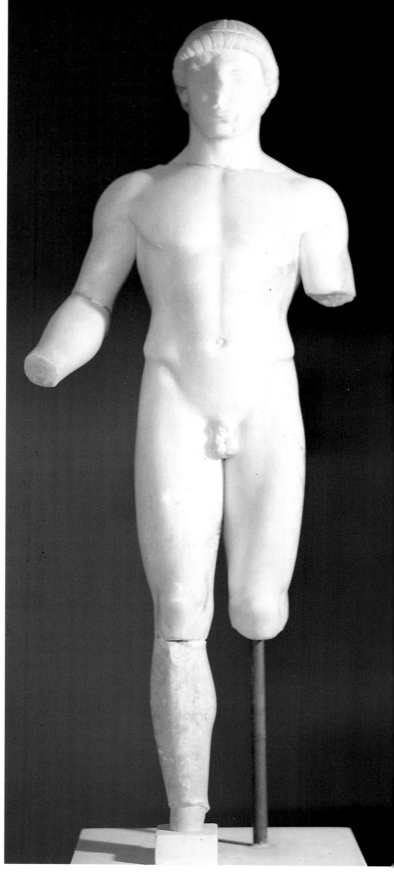

Marble statue of an **Ephebus**, an original Greek sculpture dating from the first quarter of the 5C BC and relating to the end of the Archaic age (beginning of the "severe" style). It is by some considered a marble copy of the bronze "kuros" from a Greek sanctuary (c 480 BC).

THE TEMPLE OF HERAKLES

The ruins of the **Temple of Herakles** stand high on the lower spurs of the **Hill of the Temples**, where the Byzantines cut their way through the hillside through Gate IV, leading to the road running from the emporium and cargo berth of San Leone to the Valley of the Temples, on a scenographic and fascinating spot. It was dedicated to the legendary hero (the Roman Hercules) exalted by Homer in his 15th Hymn:

> *I will sing of Heracles, the son of Zeus and much the mightest of men on earth. Alcmena bare him in Thebes, the city of lovely dances, when the dark-clouded son of Cronos had lain with her. Once he used to wander over unmeasured tracts of land and sea at the bidding of King Eurystheus, and himself did many deeds of violence and endured many: but now he lives happily in the glorious home of snowy Olympus, and has neat-ankled Hebe for his wife.*

(transl. by Hugh G. Evelyn-White, Harvard University Press)

This hero's deeds are such that the pages of our book would not suffice to tell them all, so we cannot but rely on the memory and school reminiscences of our readers.

As shown by the analyses of its remains, the temple of Herakles is the oldest of the **Agrigentine Sanctuaries**, probably erected towards the end of the 6C BC. Its attribution to Herakles is confirmed by Livy and Cicero; the latter celebrates its imposing elegance in a passage of his *Verrines*, and describes the statue in the interior: "The temple of Hercules stands on the outskirts of Agrigento, near the agora... It has the most beautiful statue I have ever seen... so beautiful that the mouth and chin are worn, as those who worship him by prayers and thanksgiving are accustomed to kissing his image."

It is a peripteral hexastyle temple, with a stylobate of 67 x 25.34 m and 38 columns, 6 on the fronts and 15 on the long sides. Together with the bronze statue of the semigod, the interior housed a painting by the famous Greek artist **Zeuxis**, which depicted Hercules' mother Alcmena assisting him in the cradle in the act of strangling the snakes sent by Hera to kill him.

MY LAST WILL AND TESTAMENT

Pass my death over
in silence.
Friends and enemies, I beg you
not to write about it in newspapers,
not to mention it at all.
No announcement, no publication.
Do not dress me when I'm dead.
Wrap me, naked, in a sheet. No flowers
on the bed, no candle burning.
A second-rate hearse, the one for the
poor. Bare.
No-one to follow, no relatives
nor friends.
Just the hearse, horse, and coachman,
no-one else.
Let my body be burnt. And, once
burnt, let it be dispersed, for
I wish nothing, not even my ashes,
to remain of me. But if that cannot
be done, then let my cinerary urn be
taken to Sicily and be embedded in some
rough stone in the country of Girgenti
where I was born.

Luigi Pirandello

*Below: The country-house where **Luigi Pirandello** was born, today a national monument housing Pirandello's Museum.*
Above: The solitary pine with the limestone block in which Pirandello's ashes are kept, the subject of a short poem: "ONE NIGHT IN JUNE/ I FELL LIKE A FIRE-FLY: BENEATH A SOLITARY PINE/ IN A COUNTRY-SIDE/ OF SARACEN OLIVE-TREES/ ON THE EDGES/ OF AN UPLAND/ OF BLUE CLAY/ OVERLOOKING THE AFRICAN SEA" (L. Pirandello).

RITORNO

Casa romita in mèzzo a la natìa
campagna, aerea qui, sull'altipìano
d'azzurre argìlle, a cui sommesso invia
fervor di spume il mare aspro africano,

te sempre vedo, sempre, da lontano,
se penso al punto in cui la vita mia
s'aprì piccola al mondo immenso e vano:
da qui – dico – da qui prèsi la via.

Da questo sentieruolo fra gli olivi,
di mentastro, di salvie profumato,
m'incamminai pe'l mondo ignaro e franco.

E tanto e tanto o fiorellini schìvi
tra l'erma siepe, tanto ho camminato
per ricondurmi a voi deluso e stanco.

Luigi Pirandello

LUIGI PIRANDELLO

Luigi Pirandello was born in Agrigento in 1867 from a wealthy bourgeois family. His interest in philology led him to attend university in Palermo, Rome and Bonn, where he took his degree in 1891 with a thesis on Greek-Sicilian dialects and worked one year as a lecturer in Italian. Back to Italy, he joined the Roman literary milieu, collaborating with the *Nuova Antologia* with poems and critical essays. Following a financial setback which affected him and his wife Antonietta Portulano, who gave him three children, Pirandello began teaching stylistics and literature at the Magistero in Rome (1897-1922).

After World War I he wrote most of the plays which were to make him famous throughout the world. From 1926 to 1934 he established a theatrical company in which Marta Abba excelled, an actress to whom he dedicated some of his plays: "Vestire gli ignudi" and "L'amica delle mogli". He became a member of the Accademia d'Italia in 1929 and won the Nobel Prize for Literature in 1934. He died in Rome in 1936, while working on his drama "I giganti della montagna". As testified by his works, including novels, plays and essays, Pirandello can be regarded as one of the foremost Italian and European authors of the early 20C.

CALTANISSETTA

The earliest historical references to Caltanissetta date from the Norman period when, in 1086, Count Roger of Hauteville occupied the territory and conquered the Pietrarossa Castle, probably an Arab stronghold. The first urban nucleus thus developed around the Norman St John's Priory. It is very interesting to visit the city's Archaeological Museum, which houses a notable collection of archaeological material discovered during excavations in the urban periphery (Monte San Giuliano) and in the archaeological sites of Capodarso, Sabucina and Gibil Gabib, from the Arab Gebel-Habib (Death Mountain), thus called for the vast necropolis with prehistoric and Greek rock-cut tombs.

Gibil-Gabib: An indigenous centre, it was first Hellenized by Gela and then by the Agrigentines in the late 6C-5C BC, during their territorial expansion over the valleys of the river Himera (now Salso) as far as the Tyrrhenian coasts. Sections of the fortified walls are still extant. The mountain was abandoned in the 4C BC.

Sabucina: Sicel indigenous centre with remains of circular huts and rock-cut chamber tombs from the early to the late Bronze Age (12C-9C BC, Pantalica culture). As the other indigenous centres in the Himera valley, in the course of the 6C BC it was occupied first by Gela and then by Agrigento, and thus Hellenized. It was abandoned at the end of the 4C BC.

Capodarso: Indigenous centre, situated 795 m above sea level on a plateau dominating the Salso valley. Based on archaeological research, it has been classified as belonging to the S. Angelo Muxaro-Polizzello cultural "facies". Hellenized during the 4C BC, it was abandoned in the early 3C BC. The necropolis has been explored and a section of the defensive works has been brought to light.

Photos: Two views of the modern city, with the expanding post-war urban quarters. Below: In the middle, the wooded hill of San Giuliano (727 m), dominating the city and its surroundings. Above: The plateau with the site of the indigenous centre of Capodarso, and the smoking peak of Mount Etna.

GELA

Founded in 689 BC by the Rhodians of Antiphemus and the Cretans of Entimus, it took its name from the nearby "Gela" river. In 580 BC Aristonous and Pystilus founded the sub-colony of Akragas (Agrigento), which soon gained independence. The first tyrant of Gela was Cleander, succeeded in 498 BC by his brother Hippocrates, who defeated the Syracusans at Helorus. When Hippocrates died in a battle against the Hyblaean Sicels, in 491 BC, he was succeeded by the tyrant Gelon, the head of Hippocrates' cavalry. After conquering Syracuse in 485 BC, he transferred a large part of the Geloan population there, leaving the city in a profound crisis which ended only after the fall of the Deinomenids in Syracuse, in 466 BC. In 424 BC a summit of Siceliot cities was held in Gela, stressing the need to send away the dangerous Athenian army, which had come to help some of them in 427 BC. The city allied with Syracuse during the Athenian expedition which ended in September 413 BC with Athen's defeat at Helorus, and with Agrigento against the Carthaginians. Beseiged by Himilco and having failed its attempt to help Dionysius I's Syracusan army, the city was captured and destroyed after a long siege, and the population deported to Leontinoi. It was repopulated under the subsequent peace treaty and compelled to demolish all its defensive works, remaining under Carthaginian and later Syracusan rule. It rose again under Timoleon in 338 BC, extending its boundary walls over the hills of Piano Soprano and Capo Notaro, where part of the fortifications are still extant. During Agathocles' tyranny in Syracuse, Gela suffered further destruction and pillage. Around 285 BC, Phintias, tyrant of Akragas, supposedly sent Mamertine mercenaries to destroy Gela and Camarina. Geloan refugees thus settled in the city of Phintias, present-day Licata.

ENNA

Because of its geographical position, almost in the centre of the island, Enna was anciently defined "umbilicus Siciliae" (the umbilicus of Sicily), as mentioned by Cicero in his *Verrines* (IV, 107). Situated in a natural strategic position at an altitude of 931 m, it was inhabited since prehistoric times, as attested by rare investigation and excavation campaigns. According to literary tradition, it was first a Sican and then a Sicel centre; in the 7C BC, it began to assimilate Greek culture through the influence of Gela and Syracuse. It was relatively independent until 396 BC, but as Syracusan interference increased, the city fell under the tyrant Dionysius the Elder. A Roman ally during the First Punic War, it was conquered by the Carthaginians in 259 BC and soon liberated, in 258 BC. But during the Second Punic War, the Roman Consul had all its citizens killed as a punishment for having allied with the Carthaginians (212 BC). It was at Enna that in 136 BC the devastating slaves' revolt led by the Syrian slave Eunus broke out, spreading throughout Sicily. Consul Rupilius besieged and reconquered the city in 132 BC, crushing any further attempt at rebellion. Also under the Romans Enna continued to be a military fortress and the administrative centre of a vast grain-producing territory. Historical sources refer to it as a "holy city" because of the cult of Ceres, the Roman goddess of fields and harvest depicted with her head wreathed in grain ears and flowers, to whom Enna dedicated statues and temples. It followed the vicissitudes of the declining Roman Empire and then passed to the Byzantines, who made it a military stronghold against Arab invasion, in view of its strategic position. After a prolonged siege, in 859 AD Enna fell and was sacked by the Muslim Abbâs Ibn Fadhl. In the 10C it became the seat of an Emirate and a Muslim stronghold against the Norman conquerors, who took it in 1087 when the Arab Hammud negotiated its surrender with Roger. During the 13C, Normans and Swabians restructured the city fortifications building the two main works, the "Lombardia Castle" and the "Old Castle", Frederick's Tower.

The city played an active role in the anti-Bourbon revolutionary movement and was among the first to rise up in the 1848-60 rebellions.

In 1926 it was raised to the status of provincial capital.

Photos: Three views of the citadel fortifications, or Lombardia Castle; the name possibly derived from a nearby Lombard quarter. An aerial view of the town showing its key strategic position, with a view of Etna in the background.

PIAZZA ARMERINA
"THE IMPERIAL VILLA DEL CASALE"

The modern town lies 721 m above sea level, on the three verdant hills dominated by the mountain on which the historic city was situated. The fertile territory has been inhabited since the 8C-7C BC, from the Greek age to the Roman and Byzantine ages and throughout the Middle Ages. Substantial evidence of settlements and necropoli has been found on the **Montagna di Marzo**, on **Monte Navone** and in **contrada Casale**. The population descends in part from the Lombard baronage who came to Sicily together with the Normans. Sharp contrasts with the Arabs who were still settled in the hamlets of the surrounding countryside during the 12C led to their annihilation which was followed, in 1161, by the destruction of the Lombard strongholds by the Norman William I the Bad in response to baronial rebellion against his centralizing power. The town was repopulated as a concession by Frederick II and a new Lombard colony was led there from Piacenza by Umberto Mostacciolo; traces of their Gallic-Italic language are still present in the local dialect. From the Monte district, the site of the first historical settlement, the town expanded over the surrounding hills between the 12C and 15C, witnessing a considerable urban development in the postwar period. In mid-August, during the two-day celebrations in honour of Maria SS. delle Vittorie, the **"Palio dei Normanni"** is held, a commemoration of the Norman victories over the Saracens, with costume parades.

THE ROMAN IMPERIAL VILLA DEL CASALE

The groups of buildings which constitute the Villa are the most notable archaeological testimonies of Roman Sicily. The luxurious manor house of Maximianus Erculeus' imperial family, situated in the fertile valley of the River Gela, was built between the end of the 3C and the early 4C AD in the middle of a vast rural latifundium. According to prof. Vinicio Gentili, the eminent researcher who discovered the archaeological site, the villa enjoyed its maximum splendour from the 4C to the 5C AD. The latifundium consisted of a rural village and of a number of "mansiones" (farms) where slaves and "procuratores" (procurators) applied themselves to exploiting the fertile land. The rooms, peristyles, arcaded courtyards and thermae are extremely interesting to visit for the splendid and incomparable series of **figured and ornamental mosaics** entirely covering the floors of the buildings.

Opposite, bottom: A general view of the buildings which constitute the Villa. Top: Panorama of present-day Piazza Armerina. On this page: The remaining marble columns of the wide arcaded atrium with entrance from three monumental doors, rather like a three-opening triumphal arch. Right: The wide peristyle surrounded by a portico, with marble columns bearing Corinthian capitals on the four sides. In the middle, the large fountain. The floor of the portico, covered with mosaics representing animals and ornamental motifs, offers a scenographic picture of life in the Roman age.

Below: Two views of the villa's thermal complex. Both the villa and Thermae were supplied by an aqueduct of which considerable traces remain. Left: The **"praefurnia"** and the **"calidaria"**, the heating system which supplied the thermae with hot water. Right: The large bath area of the thermae, an exedra with a semicircular tetrastyle portico and columns made of stuccoed circular bricks. The floor was decorated with black-and-white tesserae arranged in square patterns.

"DIAETA" OF THE LITTLE HUNT - Above: Two of the five mosaic sections depicting hunting scenes in the woods of the imperial estate. Left: The hunting of the wild boar; the animal, wounded by spears, attacks a hunter accompanied by a pack of hounds. Right: The mosaic of highest iconographic interest: In a **"lucus Dianae"**, with a column surmounted by a statue of Artemis in the middle, a sacrificial rite is performed in honour of the goddess of hunting. Below: **Cubiculum of the erotic scene**, in a perfect state of conservation. In the middle of the laurel-framed medallion, an erotic scene depicting a crowned ephebus and a half-naked maiden. For its bright colours and geometric patterns, this mosaic can be compared to the African mosaics of El-Djem, in Tunisia, as can be the medallions of the peristyle for their alternating green and red decorations and polychrome interlacements (G. V. Gentili). Right: The **"Room of the ten maidens"** (detail), with ten girls doing gymnastic exercises on a lawn, or during the prize-giving ceremony, dressed in something resembling the modern "bikini". The young girl is holding the palm of victory and wearing a wreathed crown similar to those in the mosaic depicting gladiators in the Thermae of Caracalla.

THE GREAT HUNT WALK - On these pages, the great floor mosaic in the so-called "Great Hunt" covered corridor, with details illustrating the different stages of the killing, capture and transport of animals in a typically African scenery. The corridor is delimited by two exedrae with the representation of two Roman provinces. The dark figure of Africa (Egypt or Arabia) is clearly represented by the "Phoenix", the imaginary bird which rose from its burning nest young again. In the left exedra, perhaps the representation of Armenia, flanked by a panther and a brown bear. In-between the two regions are the hunting scenes, an impressive decorative composition which surpasses the most dazzling hunting scenes in the Constantinian Villa, the numerous hunting representations discovered in Italy and Africa and the mosaics of the Imperial Palace of Constantinople, depicting similar subjects. The great, brightly figured carpet of the Villa's mosaics, while still reflecting, as a whole, the naturalistic manner, heralds the abstract colourism, opening the way to Byzantinism (G. V. Gentili). The representation of the various hunting scenes is very straightforward. Only the scene beneath Arabia is enigmatic: a winged gryphon holding a cage in its claws, with a man inside of it instead of an animal.

Above: **Vestibule of the little circus.** *Floor mosaics depicting "Children racing".*

MORGANTINA

Not far from the little town of Aidone is the archaeological site of Morgantina. According to Strabo, the city was founded by Morges, King of the Morgeti, people who arrived from southern Italy before the Greeks. The first Greek settlement dates from around the mid-6C BC, and was located on a steep hilly area (see photo opposite) dominating the underlying Agora. It seems that this first Greek settlement met with no resistance from the indigenous Morgeti and that the two cultures melted peacefully. Morgantina reached the height of its splendour around 300 BC, remaining for most of the time in the Syracusan sphere of influence; under Agathocles, the monumental Agora was restructured. Because of its opposition to the expansionist designs of the Geloan Hippocrates, it suffered the first severe destruction at the end of the 6C BC, followed in 459 BC by the raids and pillages by Ducetius' Sicels, who had united in a nationalistic movement against Greek expansion. The excavations conducted by the American Univerisity of Princeton brought to light the monumental area of the Agora and, up on the hill, the residential quarter with the ruins of luxury houses with rooms arranged around a peristyle, ornate with floor and wall decorations. According to historical sources, Morgantina was an important commercial centre in view of its geographical position on the road which, from the Sicilian Tyrrhenian coasts and from the Aeolian islands, led southwards to the city of Agira and to the southern coast of the island.

To the east of the Agora is the horseshoe theatre, dating from the 4C BC, with sixteen steps divided into five sectors. Particularly interesting is the sanctuary dedicated to Persephone and Aphrodite, as attested by terracotta offerings to Persephone and Demeter, and one to Aphrodite, unearthed in the area.

*Photos: Top, the residential quarter, the site of the archaic Greek city, on the top of the hill which was reached by means of a trapezoidal flight of steps. Bottom: A general view of the **Agora**, with the **theatre** and the Roman **gymnasium** with the rooms and basins used for ablutions. In the middle, note the flight of steps which, besides leading to the Citadel quarters, was also used for public assemblies, with a podium for speakers on the east end.*

RAGUSA

The surroundings of Ragusa Iblea bear traces of human settlements dating from as early as the 3rd millenium BC; substantial evidence has been found, in particular, of indigenous villages dating from the 9C to the 8C BC, when Greek colonization compelled the Sicels to withdraw towards the inland uplands. There they founded the city of Ibla, the **"Hibla Heraia"** mentioned by historical sources, a stronghold located on the upper Irminio valley, in a fertile land rich in water. Its proximity to the Syracusan sub-colony of Camarina, founded in 598 BC according to Thucydides, allowed Ibla to exploit the coastal trade outlets of the Greek city, establishing profitable cultural and economic relations with it. During the wearisome Punic Wars, it was conquered by the Carthaginians and later by the Romans; in the 4C AD, in view of its strategic position, it became a Byzantine stronghold surrounded by walls, but it was seized by the Muslims in 868. Under the Normans and subsequently under Manfred Chiaramonte the town's medieval layout took shape, and the Ragusa and Modica counties were united. In 1693 a devastating earthquake destroyed ancient Ibla, and a new town was built in Baroque style on the nearby Patro hill. In 1730 the medieval town of Ibla, where the most remarkable monuments of Ragusa are found, was considerably restructured by the architect Rosario Gagliardi. It is interesting to visit the Hyblaean Archaeological Museum (Museo Archeologico Ibleo), set up in 1961 to house the finds from fruitful excavations carried out throughout the Ragusan territory. The material is arranged in chronological order, from the prehistoric to the late-Roman settlements. The museum displays notable finds from archaic and classical Sicel necropoli and a rich archaeological collection of items from Hellenistic centres.

Above: A typical example of Baroque style, frequently found in public and private buildings erected after the 1693 earthquake. The balcony corbel is decorated with grotesque figures and masks, a recurrent motif in Baroque Ragusa.
Below: Panorama of Ibla, dominated by the imposing mass of the **church of San Giorgio**; *this was the site of the early Sicel settlement and later of the medieval town, restructured in 1730 to its present appearance. The Ibla urban area extends on the brow of the hill overlooking the upper Irminio valley. The visit of the old town offers the best view of the historical and artistic features of the medieval and 18C quarters.*

CHURCH OF SAN GIORGIO

It was built to the design of Rosario Gagliardo in 1738-1775, on the site of the pre-existing church of San Nicolò. The dome was built in 1820 to a design by Carmelo Cutraro.

The Latin-cross interior is divided into a nave and two aisles, with a deep apse and the transept surmounted by the slender neoclassical dome, 43 m high. The church houses some valuable paintings by Vito D'Anna over the altars and the monu-mental tomb of Bernardo Cabrera, Count of Modica and Viceroy of Sicily (1423). The sacresty houses the altar-piece in local semi-precious stone with scenes from the martyrdom of St George in the relief base. In the church treasury, a valuable Byzantine bronze reliquary framed in silver (7C), a rich Baroque ostensorium and the silver bust of St George.

CAMARINA

The third Syracusan sub-colony in order of time, Camarina was founded in 598 BC by Menecolus and Daxon. It entered into alliance with the Sicels and rebelled against its mother-town but was destroyed in 533 BC. According to Herodotus, it was conquered by the Geloan Hippocrates and rebuilt in 492 BC, but was again destroyed by Gelon, tyrant of Syracuse, who demolished the Camarina fortress and took the inhabitants to Syracuse, where they were naturalized. It was rebuilt again in 416 BC by Gela. The city remained neutral during the Peloponnesian War and took possession of Morgantina under the peace treaty signed at Gela. In the following turbulent years, it was occupied by the Carthaginians in 405 BC and was rebuilt and repopulated by Timoleon in 339 BC. It was sacked by the Syracusan general Agathocles in 309 BC and by the Mamertines in 279 BC.

The city suffered further destruction in 258 AD at the hands of the Romans and was never again rebuilt.

*Top: Panorama of ancient Ibla with the **Church of San Giorgio** and the 18C town stretching over the Patro hill.*
*Right: **San Giovanni Battista Cathedral**, built between 1706 and 1760 to a design by M. Spada and Rosario Boscarino from Modica. The two-order Baroque façade has a monumental portal in its central body.*

NOTO

Ancient Noto, a Sicel indigenous centre, was situated on the Meti hill, 152 m above sea level. It was inhabited in prehistoric times, as testified by the numerous necropoli and substantial archaeological finds from the "Castelluccio culture" (17C-15C BC) and the "Finocchito culture" (8C-7C BC). In the 3C BC, the ancient *Neai* witnessed a considerable development under Hieron I. In Roman times, it became a "civitas foederata" and enjoyed special privileges. After the Byzantine

age it was conquered by the Arabs in 866 AD, and raised to the status of capital of the Val di Noto department, becoming a rich stronghold of Muslim power in Sicily. From the 12C, under the Normans and the Swabians (except for short periods of feudal submission), it was a city of the royal domain, entrusted with the administration of vast territories, and as such it enjoyed considerable economic and commercial prosperity. Talented men of culture were born in Noto, such as the humanist Giovanni Aurispa, the architect Matteo Carnelivari and

the jurist Andrea Barbagio. In the 16C and 17C the transformation of the medieval town began, but was suddenly interrupted by the 1693 earthquake.
Following the disastrous event, Giuseppe Lanza, Duke of Camastra and royal official in charge of the reconstruction work, decided to build the new town on a different site. Renowned architects and engineers participated in the construction of the new town, including Rosario Gagliardi, Paolo Labisi, Vincenzo Sinatra, Antonio Mazza and a skilful group of master stonecutters who, in the course of the 18C, created an extraordinary urban and monumental site of outstanding artistic value.

*In the photos: above, the **"Chiesa Madre"**, the main church, begun in the early 18C and completed in 1776. Opposite: The **church of San Francesco**, the work of the architect Rosario Gagliardi, and the side of the **Santissimo Salvatore convent**, with its pointed tower, creating a scenographic ensemble of great architectural value from the top of the monumental steps.*

SYRACUSE

Archaeological investigation has found human traces dating from as early as the 14C BC on the *island of Ortygia*, the site on which the great city of Syracuse was to be founded in the 8C BC. The new settlement was established by the Corinthians led by Archias, driving the previous settlers, the Sicels, back towards the Hyblaean Mountains; it took its name from a nearby marsh called Syrako. The new settlers embarked on a programme of economic and political development and territorial expansion which, in a 70-year period, led to the foundation of three colonies: *Akrai* in 664 BC (present-day Palazzolo Acreide), *Casmene* in 643 BC and *Camarina*, on the southern coast of the island, in 598 BC.

THE GREEK THEATRE

Hieron II had it built on the site of a pre-existing theatre whose history is associated with *Aeschylus* of Eleusis (c 524-456 BC), the first of the great Greek tragedicians, *Epicharmus* (6C-5C BC), the Syracusan father of Greek comedy, and their contemporaries *Phormides* and *Deinolochus*. This earlier theatre witnessed the premiere of Aeschylus' tragedy "The Persians" and, in 476 BC, "The Women of Etna", written to celebrate the foundation of Etna by Hieron I the Etnean. The name of the architect who built this earlier theatre, Demokopos, has been handed down to us by the mime-writer Sophron (late 5C BC). In Roman times the theatre was altered so as to adapt it to the performance of circus and water games. During the reign of Charles V, the ancient stones of the theatre, amphitheatre and the Altar of Hieron II were used to build the fortifications on the island of Ortygia, suffering the same fate as many other noble monuments of ancient Sicily.

Strabo, the Greek historian and man of letters born in Amasea, Pontus (c 64 BC), who spent long years in Rome during the first Imperial Age between Augustus and Tiberius, thus wrote about the foundation of Syracuse in his valuable treatise of Italic geography: "Syracuse was founded by Archias, who sailed from Corinth about the same time that Naxos and Megara were colonised. It is said that **Archias** went to Delphi at the same time as **Myscellus**, and when they were consulting the oracle, the god asked them whether they chose wealth or health; now Archias chose wealth, and Myscellus health; accordingly, the god granted to the former to found Syracuse, and to the latter Croton. And it actually came to pass that the Crotoniates took up their abode in a city that was exceedingly healthful, as I have related, and that Syracuse fell into such ex-

Right: Roman tomb with overhang, known as the tomb of **Archimedes**. *Below: The* **Altar of Hieron II**, *a monumental altar for public sacrifices built in the 3C BC and dedicated to Zeus Eleutherios. Its proportions are majestic, being 198 m long and 22.80 m wide.*
Opposite page: The modern statue of Archimedes, the great Syracusan mathematician and physicist (287-212 BC), killed by a Roman soldier during the siege laid by the Roman Consul Marcellus.

ceptional wealth that the name of the Syracusans was spread abroad in a proverb applied to the excessively stravagant - "The tithe of the Syracusans would not be sufficient for them". [...] And the city grew, both on account of the fertility of the soil and on account of the natural excellence of its harbours. Furthermore, the men of Syracuse proved to have the gift of leadership, with the result that when the Syracusans were ruled by tyrants they lorded it over the rest, and when set free themselves they set free those who were oppressed by the barbarians". (Strabo, *Geography, Italy*: VI, 2. 3-4, transl. by H.L. Jones, Harvard University Press)
Historical references to the period following the foundation of the city, up to the early 5C BC, have been lost. During this obscure period, political power was wielded by the "gamoroi", aristocrats and landowners, expelled by a popular democratic revolt at the beginning of the 5C BC. The city's great historical epoch began when Gelon, of the Deinomenids of Gela, came to power; he provided for the return of the aristocrats and set himself at the head of the Greek settlements of Sicily against the Carthaginians, who aimed at conquering the whole island. Under Hieron I, the city grew more powerful and consolidated its supremacy over the western Mediterranean following the naval victory off Cumae in 474 BC over the Etruscans.

THE ROMAN AMPHITHEATRE

This majestic construction, dating from the 4C-3C BC, is one of the largest among the late-Roman Amphitheatres of Catania, Pompei and Pola. Elliptical in plan, it measures 140 x 119 m in the external diameter and 70 x 40 m in the arena, with a central cistern supplied by two canals. Its lower part was carved from the rock, according to Syracusan tradition. The steps were originally lined with slabs of stone, in order to prevent rock deterioration. At the ends of the long axis, two entrances led into the arena, the main entrance being originally to the right. At the foot of the steps there was a vaulted corridor for the entrance of wild animals and gladiators taking part in the bloody performances held in the arena.

THE EAR OF DIONYSIUS

This artificial cave, 65 m long and 23 m high, was given its name by **Michelangelo Merisi**, known as **Caravaggio**, when in 1586, accompanied by the Syracusan archaeologist Vincenzo Mirabella, he visited the **Latomie del Paradiso** and the cave, noting the human ear-shaped entrance to the latter. The legend was thus created that Dionysius had the cave excavated to use it as a prison and exploited its still amazing acoustics to eavesdrop on his prisoners.

THE TEMPLE OF APOLLO
(Apolloyon)

Dating from the early 6C BC, it is considered the oldest Doric peripteral temple in Sicily. It measures 58.10 x 24.50 m, with 17 columns on the long sides and 6 on the fronts. The cella was divided into aisles by two rows of double-order columns. Its archaic character is attested by the design of the columns and by the width of the intercolumns.

In the course of the centuries, the temple has been altered and adapted.

In Byzantine times, it was a Christian church; it was a Mosque under the Muslims, and a Norman basilica in the Middle Ages; later, in the 16C, it was a Spanish barracks known as the "Old Quarter".

THE CATHEDRAL (Duomo)

The Christian basilica was built in the 7C on the site of the pre-existing temple of Athena. Ten Doric columns of the temple, which was erected by the Deinomenids, are embedded in the walls of the left nave. The Cathedral façade, destroyed by the 1693 earthquake, was rebuilt in 1725-1753 to a design by Andrea de Palma.

*Above: The spire of the sanctuary of the **Madonna delle Lacrime**, 94.30 m high, dominating all the other city buildings and fully visible from long distances. On the top, the golden statue of the Virgin Mary surrounded by the rays of the Holy Spirit.*

Eighteen entrances lead into the Crypt, which can contain 3,000 people. The reinforced concrete structure of the church, 74.30 m high, covers an area of 4,700 sq m for a total capacity of 11,000.

THE SANCTUARY OF THE MADONNA DELLE LACRIME

One morning, on 29 August 1953, a small plaster image of the Virgin Mary in the house of Angelo Iannuso and Antonina Giusto suddenly began to shed tears. The following days, on 30 and 31 August and on 1 September, tears were seen again on the Virgin's face. This extraordinary phenomenon turned the house of the two simple workers into a sort of sanctuary, attracting an increasing multitude of people anxious to see and touch the tears coming out from the Virgin's clear eyes. A commission appointed by the archiepiscopal Curia ascertained the tears to be human; on 19 May 1954, Cardinal Ruffini, the Archbishop of Palermo, laid the foundation-stone of the present Sanctuary of the Madonna delle Lacrime (Our Lady of the Tears), built by two French architects, Michel Andrault and Pierre Parat.

On 29 August 1968, the sacred image of the Virgin was displayed in the Crypt, which was opened on 1 September. Now it is exhibited in the higher part of the building, completed in 1990.

*In piazza della Vittoria, to the south of the sanctuary of the Madonna delle Lacrime, archaeological excavations have brought to light a vast complex of ancient buildings, dating from the 6C-5C to the Byzantine age. Of particular interest is the **sanctuary of Demeter and Kore**, mentioned by literary tradition. The measures of a temple (10 x 18 m) have been derived from the foundations. In the surroundings, a sacrificial altar and a votive stipe with clay statuettes of Demeter or Kore, holding the symbols of divinity, the torch and the piglet, in their hands.*

THE CIANE SPRING

The banks of the mythical river Ciane, gushing out from the spring bearing the same name (Fonte Ciane), offer a peculiar and delightful itinerary on foot or by boat among the lush vegetation of papyrus plants, ash-trees and willows growing naturally for seven kilometres from the source to the mouth of the river. The Greek name derives from the colour of its waters (cyanos-blue) or, more poetically, from the myth of Cyane, daughter of Cyanippus, Bacchus' priest in Syracuse, who was with Proserpina the day in which the latter was abducted by Pluto. The god of the Underworld punished Cyane for having tried to prevent the rape of Proserpina by turning her into a spring. In 1984, a Natural Oriented Reserve was set up, expanding the Natural Reserve created in 1981, with a view to preserving the environmental richness of the territory, a unique example in Europe in that the papyrus still grows wild in the magic atmosphere of the Greek mythical world. In the photos, two views of the luxuriant banks of the river.

THE FOUNTAIN OF ARETHUSA

"August resting-place of Alpheus
flower of the illustrious Syracuse, Ortygia".
(Pindar)

Thus the poet sang the famous myth of Arethusa, nymph of Artemis and daughter of Nereus and Doris, whom a legend associates to the origins of Syracuse: "One day Arethusa, searching refreshment from hunting, bathed in the river Alpheus whom, struck by love for the beautiful nymph, took on human form to pursue her. In order to protect Arethusa, Artemis turned her into a spring, flowing undergound to emerge on the islet of Ortygia". The head of Arethusa, surrounded by darting dolphins, is a recurrent motif on the coins minted in Syracuse. Opposite, the silver tetradachm with the signature of the engraver, Kimon, and the image of the Medusa. The legend highlights the ethnic and religious link between Syracuse and its mother-city, Corinth. Since ancient times, the site has been a source of inspiration for many travellers and men of letters. Publius Vergilius Maro, the great Latin writer and poet from Andes, near Mantova (70-19 BC), also sang the fountain in his verses:

"Right o'er against Plemmyrium's wat'ry strand,
there lies an isle once call'd the Ortygian land.
Alpheus, as old fame reports, has found
from Greece a secret passage under ground,
by love to beauteous Arethusa led;
and, by mingling here, they roll in the same sacred bed.
As Helenus enjoin'd, we next adore
Diana's name, protectress of the shore.
With prosp'rous gales we pass the quiet sound
of still Elorus, and his fruitful bounds".
(Virgil; Aeneid, book III-151, transl. by J. Dryden, The Harvard Classics).

*Below: **The Fountain of Arethusa** with the luxuriant papyrus plants, attracting the attention of numerous tourists.*

THE CASTLE OF EURYALUS

It took its name from the morphology of the land on which it was erected (Euryalus = Eurvelos, broad-based nail). The great archaeological site is one of the most extraordinary examples of ancient Greek military architecture. The area, situated on the highest point of the Epipolae, was crossed by the road which linked Syracuse to its inland territories. During the Athenian siege (415-413 BC), the plateau had not been fortified yet and represented one of the weak points of the Syracusan defensive system. It was on this occasion that the need was felt to build a powerful stronghold in order to protect the city against enemy attacks. The chronological order of the construction work has not been confirmed by archaeological research. This extraordinary defensive bulwark, against which the power of the Carthaginian army shattered, was built by Dionysius the Elder in six years, from 402 to 397 BC.

Top: One of the three moats with the piers supporting the wooden bridge linking the main body. Bottom: The courtyard, the heart of the defensive system, with three of the five original towers. From the vast square, surrounded by various buildings, a series of underground passages enabled soldiers to make sorties outside when necessary. In the course of the centuries, the fortress underwent several alterations in order to adapt it to the new defensive systems, until the Roman conquest in 212 BC. In Byzantine times, it was partly rebuilt to protect the city against Arab attacks.

THE TEMPLE OF OLYMPIAN JUPITER
On the right bank of the river Ciane are the two extant Doric fluted columns of the temple dedicated to the Lord of Olympus. Built in the early 6C BC, it was a Doric peripteral hexastyle temple, with 42 columns, 6 on the fronts and 17 on the long sides.

THE ROMAN GYMNASIUM
The monumental complex known as Gymnasium, probably built in the second half of the 1C AD, consists of various constructions. Surrounded by the remains of a quadriportico are the ruins of a temple preceded by an altar, and a theatre. There was also, from Greek times, the sacellum with the remains of Timoleon.

The "Paolo Orsi"
REGIONAL ARCHAEOLOGICAL MUSEUM

The Museum is dedicated to Paolo Orsi, the great archaeologist from Rovereto, Trento (1859-1935). An expert of Hellenic and pre-Hellenic civilisations, he worked for years in Sicily; in Syracuse, he arranged the first Archaeological Museum in Piazza Duomo, a task which was later continued by another great archaeologist, Bernabò Brea, in the post-war period. As the exhibition space proved insufficient to house all the material from the great investigation and excavation campaigns in the main archaeological sites of eastern Sicily, the new Museum was begun in 1967, with financial support from the Development Fund for Southern Italy (Cassa del Mezzogiorno) and the Regional Ministry for Cultural and Environmental Heritage, and opened in 1988.

Built in the park of Villa Landolina by the architect Franco Minissi, it is the most important and innovative museum in Sicily, and one of the foremost in Europe. In its 9,000 sq m of exhibition space on two floors, the Museum displays 18,000 archaeological finds from the city of Syracuse and from the eastern regions of the island.

Above: One of the Attic vases from the necropoli, black- and red-figured and datable from the 5C BC. The vases provide valuable information on Greek ceramics ranging from the 8C BC to the Hellenistic age.

Right: Small bronze of an offering athlete holding a phiale in his right hand, from Mendolito, near Adrano, probably a smaller copy of a great votive statue; attributed to Pythagoras of Rhegium (c 460 BC).

*Below: Limestone **"Kourotrophos"**, a headless goddess breast-feeding two twins with adult faces. From Megara Hyblaea, northern necropolis (550 BC).*

Below: Bronze head of Medusa, from Palazzolo Acreide (mid-2C BC).

The Museum extends horizontally and is arranged on two floors. It houses 3,000 sq m of storerooms and laboratories in the basement, and the exhibition rooms on the upper floor. In the central body, a hall leads into the Auditorium, equipped with modern audiovisual systems for the projection of films and slides, and also used for cultural and information activities.

The chronological succession of exhibits in the various sectors starts from the prehistoric and protohistoric ages, from the Paleolithic to the Neolithic, and continues with the Copper Age and different stages of the Bronze (early, middle, late and last) and Iron Ages. The following sector displays material from the first Greek colonies of Naxos, Mylai, Zancle, Katane and Leontinoi, the largest space being devoted to the Doric colonies of Megara Hyblaea and Syracuse. Of extreme historical and artistic interest are the tomb furnishings from the Syracusan necropoli, with a vast collection of Corinthian, Ionic, Rhodian, Attic and Etruscan imported pottery. Next are the architectural terracottas from the urban and extra-urban sanctuaries of Syracuse, from the temple of Apollo, the Athenaion, the Ciane Sanctuary, the temple of Apollo Temenites, the two sanctuaries of Artemis at Scala Greca and Belvedere and the temple of Olympian Zeus on the banks of the Anapo. There is a rich collection of religious terracottas manufactured in Siceliot workshops in the 5C and 4C BC, from Gela, Agrigento, Camarina and other eastern sites of the island.

*Detail of a bright polychrome terracotta frieze with the **Gorgon** (first half of the 6C BC). Below: Aerial photo of the **"Paolo Orsi" Museum**, with its characteristic daisy-shaped layout, in the park of Villa Landolina.*

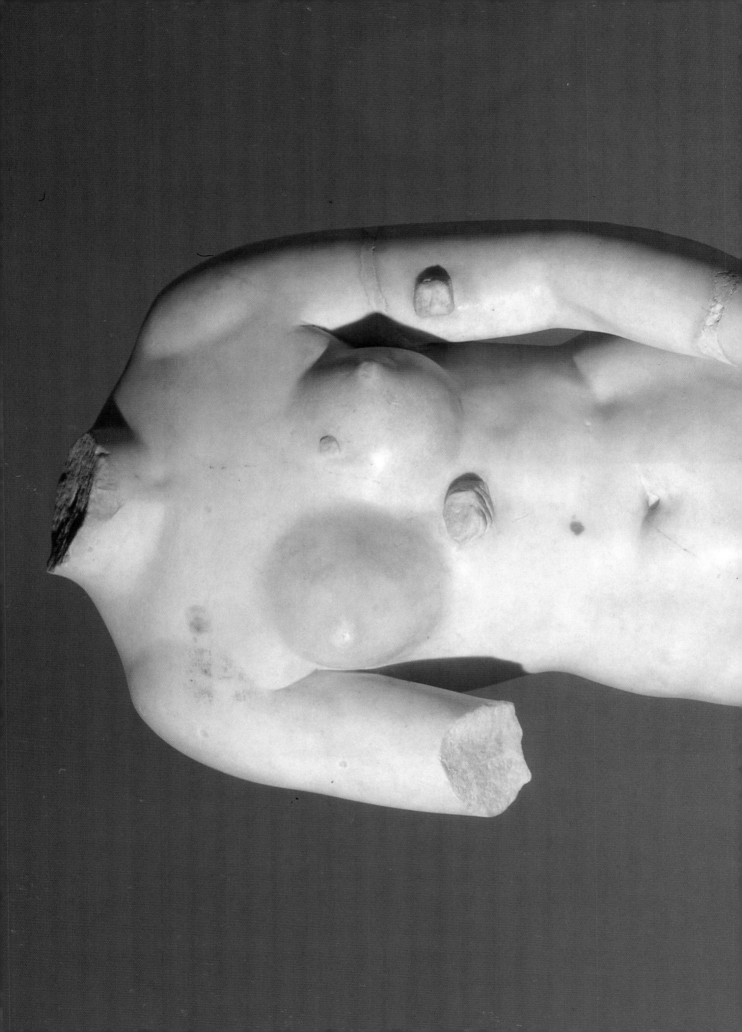

Gorgon from the Temple of Athena, Syracuse, 570-550 BC.

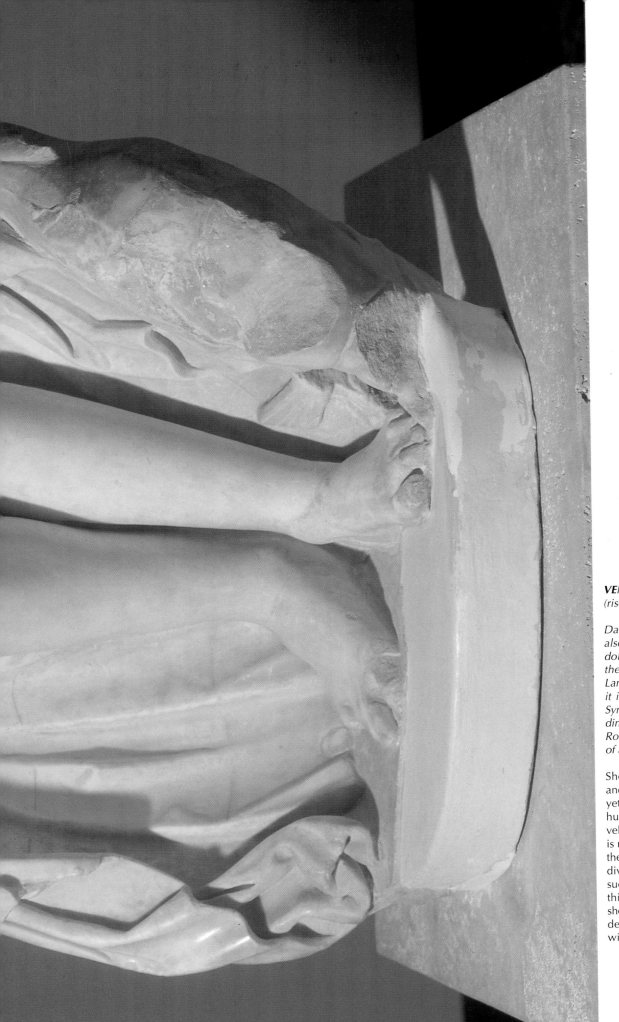

VENUS ANADYOMENE
(risen from the sea)

Dating from the 2C AD, also known as "Venus Landolina" from the name of the archaeologist Saverio Landolina, who discovered it in a nymphaeum in the Syracusan quarter of Achradina. The marble statue is a Roman-Imperial imitation of a Rhodian original.

She hasn't got the head, and an arm is missing; and yet, I have never found the human figure more marvellous and seductive. This is not the woman of poets, the idealized woman, the divine or majestic woman such as the Venus de Milo, this is the woman just as she is, the way we love her, desire her, the way we wish to hold her.

(Guy de Maupassant)

AUGUSTA

The island of Augusta, linked to the mainland by two bridges, has always served as a key stronghold and military base since the 13C, when Frederick II of Swabia built its fortifications to protect the eastern coast of Sicily and enlarged it with the inhabitants of the nearby cities which had rebelled against him and thus been destroyed.

During the 14C, it was torn by the rivalry between Aragonese and Angevins for its possession. It was occupied by Frederick of Aragon, who later yielded it to Count Moncada di Montecateno (16C). In order to protect it against Muslim and other Berber attacks, the Forts of Vittoria and Garcia were built by Viceroy Garcia of Toledo, and Fort Avalos by Marquis Ferdinando Avalos of Pescara. In 1676 it suffered severe damage from the bloody struggles opposing the Spanish and the French, but it was rebuilt and fortified with new boundary walls by the Viceroy Benavides. Completely destroyed by the 1693 earthquake, it was soon rebuilt. Augusta, which is still a military port, has witnessed a considerable maritime trade development following coastal industrialization, with the establishment of huge petrochemical plants. Of particular interest is the small peninsula of Brucoli, where traces of Neolithic and early Bronze Age settlements have been found.

PALAZZOLO ACREIDE (Akrai)

Substantial traces of human settlements from prehistoric times have been found in the surroundings of the present-day town. In 664 BC Syracuse, pursuing its vehement expansionist policy towards the hinterland, founded its first sub-colony, Akrai. The road which led to the new city was of vital strategic importance for the communications between Syracuse and the Greek cities on the southern coast via the Selinuntine road. After 214 BC, it became a Roman "Civitas stipendiaria" and continued to flourish thanks to the fertile agricultural land. Probably destroyed by the Greeks, it was reconquered in Norman times. Archaeological excavations in ancient Akrai have brought to light the Greek theatre (photo above) dating from the 3C BC, a rather small though well preserved building, with a semicircular cavea divided into 9 wedges and 12 steps which could seat 600 people. Photo below: The Latomie dell'Intagliata and dell'Intagliatella, stone quarries from the Greek age with rock carvings, which were used for hero-worship. The foundations of a Greek-archaic temple, probably dedicated to Aphrodite, stand high above the Latomie.

CATANIA

"Thucles and the Chalcidians set out from Naxos five years after the foundation of Syracuse, drove out the Sicels by arms and founded Leontini and afterwards Catania, the Catanians themselves choosing Evarchus as their founder".

(Thucydides, book VI, 3)

We thus learn that Katane was founded by Chalcidian colonists shortly after 729 BC, during the earliest stage of Greek colonization in Sicily. The territory was previously inhabited by the Sicels from central and southern Italy who, during the Bronze Age, had in turn driven Sican settlers westwards. Katane and the other Chalcidian cities, founded in the valley crossed by the Simeto river, lived in harmony with each other and with the Sicel populations of the surrounding territories, until Hieron I, tyrant of Syracuse, came to power. In 476 BC, he transplanted the populations of Naxos and Katane to Leontini and "re-founded" Katane under a new name, Etna, bringing settlers from the Peloponnese, and introducing his son Deinomenes as its ruler. This tragic event provided the main theme for Pindar's "First Pithian" and was also celebrated by Aeschylus in his play "The Women of Etna", unfortunately lost (c 470 BC). In 461 BC, following a Sicel-Syracusan attack, the population of Etna was forced to seek refuge in Sicel territory, at Inessa, which was renamed Etna. Katane, repopulated by Hieron's expellees and by the new Syracusan and Sicel settlers, was restored to its original name. A great figure, though one that is somewhat tinged with legend, was the Catanian lawgiver Charondas, who lived in an uncertain age (probably, based on an assumption, between the end of the 7C and the beginning of the 6C BC), the author of a written law code which was to be accepted in other Greek-Sicilian cities of Chalcidian origin. In 263 BC, during the Second Punic War, Katane was conquered by the Romans and renamed Catina. After 210 BC, as the Roman conquest of the island was complete, the devastated cities and countryside called for quick and extensive reconstruction. The "Roman Pax" immediately succeeded in achieving this goal, and throughout the Republican and Imperial ages "Catina" became a prosperous city, as attested by both historical sources and the considerable number of Roman buildings that have been brought to light, though, as noted by the Christian historian P. Orosio, the city was destroyed in 123 by a terrible eruption.

*Above: The **Swabian Castello Ursino**, housing the **Civic Museum**. Built by Frederick II of Swabia between 1239 and 1250, under the supervision of the royal fortification superintendent, Riccardo Lentini. The castle originally rose on a promontory, but a lava mass from the 1669 eruption separated it from the coast. A royal residence under the Aragonese, it was restored with Renaissance alterations.*

*Left: Aerial view of the city centre, with the **church of San Francesco** (in the foreground) and, above, the imposing mass of the **Cathedral** and the dome of **Sant'Agata Abbey**, built by G.B. Vaccarini in 1735-67.*

*Right: The monumental façade of the **church of San Nicolò**, begun in 1687 by G.B. Contini. The construction was repeatedly discontinued and resumed for various reasons until 1796, when C. Battaglia Sant'Angelo started work again, however leaving it incomplete. Today it is used as a "Chapel to the Fallen".*
The Latin-cross interior, divided into a nave and two aisles by massive columns and paired pilaster-strips, covers an area of 105 x 48 m (as far as the transept), reaching the dizzy height of 62 m in the dome.

THE ROMAN THEATRE

It was built at the foot of the ancient Greek Acropolis, presumably on the site of an earlier Greek theatre, though the hypothesis has not been confirmed by archaeological investigation as its structure essentially dates from Roman times. Excavations carried out in the 18C brought to light architectural marble fragments from the stage, stone inscriptions and remains of statues, now exhibited in the Civic Museum housed at Castello Ursino. The theatre, which could seat about 7,000 people, had a diameter of 87 m (29 m in the orchestra). The cavea, divided into 9 wedges with a two-stepped enclosure, was surrounded by three ambulatories, the higher and more imposing of which formed the base of the flight of steps of the "summa cavea".

Water from the subterranean course of the Amenano river often comes up through the ground in the orchestra, forming a pool and flooding the structures. Excavations recently carried out in the stage area have brought to light some columns, a statue and remains of the stage itself, with niches and marble facings.

Top: The orchestra, with the foundations flooded by the waters of the Amenano.
*Bottom: The external wall of the **"Odeon"**, a small circular theatre with a seating capacity of 1,300, divided into non-communicating spaces, with the entrances to the portico leading into the upper ambulatory of the Theatre. Opposite, the cavea of the Roman Theatre.*

The remains of the Theatre (with a seating capacity of 7,000) and of the Amphitheatre (15,000), as well as the ruins of an odeon, the Forum, thermal baths and an aqueduct, all testify to the wealth of the Roman city, particularly during the Augustan age, when it was assigned the special status of colony. The early spread of Christianity in Sicily, which was still religiously dominated by the syncretism of the late-Hellenistic world, was marked by the slow transition to the Word of Christ and by the martyrdom of the first Christians, including,

in Catania, St Euplus and St Agatha, the future patron saint of the city. Following the disintegration of the Roman Empire caused by the Barbarian invasions, the city and its activities began to decline. In a letter written by Cassiodorus, the Goth king Theodoric reportedly authorized the Catanians to use the stones of the amphitheatre to restore the city walls. In 535 AD Catania was reconquered by the Byzantine Belisarius, and later passed to Muslim rule during the 9C. Roger I of Hauteville conquered the city in 1071, driving out the Arabs.

THE ROMAN AMPHITHEATRE

A huge construction dating from the Imperial age, probably from the 2C AD. Elliptic in plan, it measures 125 m and 105 m in the major and minor axes, respectively, and is second in size only to the Colosseum, with an arena measuring 71 x 51 m. It had 32 tiers of seats, for a total capacity of about 16,000. In the photo: **Piazza Stesicoro**, with the ruins of the Amphitheatre. The steps were cut out of lava stone, and part of the building was faced with marble and granite.

Left: The well-preserved lower portico with part of the vault. In the background, the façade of the church of **Sant'Agata alla Fornace** (early 18C), built on the site where, according to tradition, St Agatha was martyred. The church is neoclassical in style, the work of Antonino Battaglia.

Opposite page: Aerial view of **piazza del Duomo**, the square with the Cathedral dedicated to St Agatha, the Elephant fountain and the octagonal dome of Sant'Agata Abbey by Vaccarini.

Bottom: The back of **"Palazzo Biscari"** overlooking the sea. The balcony is decorated with caryatids and windows framed by putti and festoons, an 18C masterpiece by Antonino Amato. In the magnificent rooms, Prince Ignazio Paternò Castello displayed a rich collection of archaeological finds which was later to be transferred to Castello Ursino.

The remains of a Roman building found in the underground have traditionally been considered to be the ruins of St Agatha's birthplace. Palazzo Biscari was designed in the early 18C by Alonzo Benedetto and Giuseppe Palazzotto, who built the east wing in 1750. It was modified in 1763 to a design by Francesco Battaglia, and completed by his son Antonino. The interior is sumptuous, with a succession of rooms decorated with frescoes and Rococo polychrome encrustations. The "ball room", decorated with mirrors, was frescoed in 1766 by Sebastiano Lo Monaco.

THE CATHEDRAL

It was built between 1078 and 1093 by the Norman Count Roger of Hauteville, on the site and remains of the Roman Imperial "Thermae of Achilles". It was originally a fortified church ("ecclesia munita"), as attested by the transept, with its scattered single- and double-light windows, and by the battlemented top. Material from Roman Imperial buildings was used for its construction.

The main body and the façade were designed by Giovan Battista Vaccarini and built between 1733 and 1761. The dome was built in the last decade of the 18C to a design by Antonio Battaglia. The bell tower, built in 1868 by Carmelo Sciuto Patti, is a reconstruction of the 15C original, which collapsed upon the naves during the 1693 earthquake. The reconstruction project was by the architect Girolamo Palazzotto. The church was restored at the end of the 1950s by the architect Raffaele Leone. The interior, divided by pillars into a nave and two aisles, reflects the reconstruction work by Girolamo Palazzotto. Of the original Norman architecture, the transept and apses remain. Placed against one of the pillars of the nave is the monumental tomb with the remains of the great Catanian composer **Vincenzo Bellini**, transferred there in 1876 from the Père Lachaise cemetery in Paris; the tomb is the work of Giovan Battista Tassara. The cathedral is rich in works of art and historical relics of the city. It is dedicated to St Agatha, a Catanian virgin martyred in 250 AD under the Emperor Decius. Every year, on 5 November, a solemn ceremony is held in her honour. In the sacellum of the right apse are the **relics** of the saint and the valuable **"treasury of St Agatha"**, including the outstanding "Shrine", a large reliquary in embossed wrought silver decorated with statues of saints, a fine example of Sicilian "gothique flamboyant" designed and executed by Antonio La Nuara in 1460-76, resumed and completed in 1572 by Sicilian artists such as Lattari, De Mauro, P. Guarna, Vincenzo and Antonino Archifel.

*Photo: The **Cathedral** and the **Elephant fountain**, designed by G.B. Vaccarini in 1736 after Bernini's elephant in Piazza della Minerva, in Rome. The base on which the Elephant stands is decorated with sculptured allegories of the Catanian rivers Simeto and Amenano and with putti pouring water into the underlying basins. Above the elephant is an obelisk with hieroglyphs referring to the cult of Isis, possibly a "goal" from the Roman Imperial circus of Catania.*

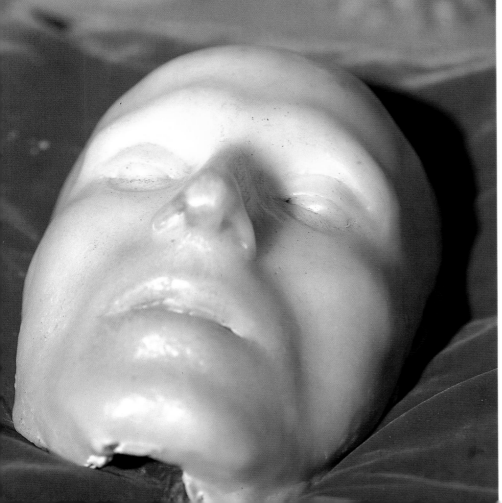

THE VINCENZO BELLINI MUSEUM

The house where Catania's illustrious child was born and lived his adolescence is now a museum with mementos and relics relating to his life and work.

Vincenzo Bellini was born in Catania in 1801 from Rosario and Agata Ferlito. His first teacher was his father, an organist, choir-master and sacred music composer; at the very early age of 6, he composed his first piece, showing a real talent for music. His paternal grandfather Vincenzo Tobia, he himself an organist and composer, was also his teacher.

Very soon, as a young boy, he displayed his versatile gift for music composing sacred and secular pieces which he played on church organs and in the "high-society" salons of the city. The Commune of Catania, in 1819, financed his studies at the conservatory of Naples by granting him a scholarship.

In Naples he had important maestros as his teachers, such as Furno, G. Tritto and Zingarelli. He continued to compose chamber and sacred music, and published his first work, a romanza entitled "Dolente Immagine". In 1825 he completed his studies by composing, as a final piece, the semiseria "Adelson e Salvini", which was so successful that he was commissioned to write an opera for the San Carlo Theatre: "Bianca e Fernando" (1826). The following year, he was engaged by the theatrical impresario Domenico Barbaja and composed "Il Pirata" for La Scala in Milan, a work in which the features of his operatic production are first reflected. In 1827, his unsuccessful love for Maddalena Fumaroli led him to settle in Milan, where he began a fruitful collaboration with the librettist Felice Romani which was to last until his penultimate work, "Beatrice di Tenda". His immortal works were all composed in eight years, from 1827 to 1835, when, after a short stay in London, he died in Paris of an intestinal disease which had long been afflicting him. A musical genius of the Italian Romanticism, Bellini thus wrote of himself:

"...I have resolved to write few scores, no more than one a year, and I shall dedicate myself entirely to these, as I am convinced that their success will depend in large part on the choice of a captivating subject, on warm expression, on the conflict of passions".

Bellini's works, known and performed all over the world, show his expressive strength and his ability to reconcile the rules of classical melody with a passionate lyric and poetic emphasis, producing an amazingly beautiful result. This is also evident in his "I Puritani" which, in the "Suoni la tromba e intrepido", conveys the new awareness of the Italian Risorgimento, the main theme of the work which was to be defined "the Italian Marseillaise".

After "Il Pirata" (1827), Bellini composed "La Straniera" (1829), "I Capuleti e i Montecchi" (1830), "La Sonnambula" (1831), "Norma" (1832) and "I Puritani" (1835), shortly before his death.

*Above: Oil-painting of **Bellini** as a youth. Opposite page: An autograph score by the maestro placed on the music-stand of the harpsichord probably used by his grandfather Vincenzo Tobia for Bellini's first music lessons. Bottom: **The wax funeral mask** reproduced from the original cast.*

Above: The alcove in Room B of the Museum, where Vincenzo Bellini was born in 1801. It houses the harpsichord on which Bellini performed his "Norma" during his stay in Catania in 1832.
Below: Room C with the wall showcases exhibiting a rich iconographic collection related to Bellini's life, autograph letters, and the original documents regarding his death at Puteaux, the death certificate and the med-
ical post-mortem report. There is also a collection of portraits of orchestra conductors, famous interpreters such as Malibran and Turina, relatives and friends of the great Maestro. Room D displays the autograph scores of Bellini's works from 1811 to 1818, sacred and secular music composed during his studies at the Conservatory in Naples.

Bellini's memorabilia are displayed in three communicating rooms on the entresol of Palazzo Gravina, the composer's birthplace, constituting the **Vincenzo Bellini Museum**.
The Museum houses the Maestro's iconographic collection, with an outstanding lifelike portrait by Natale Schiavoni (1830). Room D displays the autograph scores of various works, including "Adelson e Salvini", "I Capuleti e i Montecchi", the adaptation of "I Puritani" for Maria Malibran and the unfinished "Ernani".

Room B with the wall showcases displaying the Bellinian iconographic collection, various portraits of the Maestro and his parents, and the documents relating to the resolutions which the Commune of Catania passed in his favour: the scholarship, and the building of a memorial in Piazza Stesicoro, the work of Giulio Monteverde (1882).

The central showcase exhibits personal belongings, the wax funeral mask, a miniature portrait by Maria Malibran and a tiny self-portrait of the singer. Adjoining the Museum are the centre of Bellinian studies and the Music Library.

THE EMILIO GRECO MUSEUM

The Museum is dedicated to the great sculptor born in Catania, and exhibits some of his works. Greco's art draws inspiration from Roman portraiture and Etruscan terracottas, in the framework of the naturalistic figurative sculptural tradition which, towards the late 1920s, was enriched with classical and archaic expressive forms inspired by Etruscan sculpture; a school represented by such artists as Pericle Fazzini, Marino Marini, Giacomo Manzù, Francesco Messina and Luciano Minguzzi.

His works are influenced by Francesco Laurana, one of the foremost sculptors and architects of the Renaissance (bust of Eleanor of Aragon, Palermo National Gallery), and later by Mannerism. Female nudes and portrait busts are among his recurrent themes. His works include the bronze gates of the Orvieto Cathedral (1961-64); the monument dedicated to Pinocchio at Collodi (1954) and the monument to Pope John XXIII in St Peter's Basilica, Rome (1965-67).

TEATRO MASSIMO VINCENZO BELLINI

The main opera house in Catania, dedicated to Vincenzo Bellini, was inaugurated on 31 May 1890 with the performance of Bellini's "Norma". In 1812, the construction was first commissioned to the Maltese architect Zahara Buda. Work was started but was then interrupted following various events, and the sum appropriated for the theatre was allocated for the building of an outer breakwater in the port of Catania, to protect it against the frequent Algerian piratical raids in the Ionian Sea. Having lost the traces of the first project, in 1841 a new project was commissioned by the Senate of Catania to the architect Carlo Sama. The theatre undoubtedly reflects Sama's eclecticism and archi-

tectural elegance both from the decorative and the functional-acoustic points of view. The magnificent hall has four tiers of boxes and a gallery with a frescoed ceiling, the work of Ernesto Bellandi depicting Bellini's Apotheosis and allegories of his Norma, I Puritani, La Sonnambula and Il Pirata. The curtain, by G. Sciuti, celebrates the victory of the Catanians over the Libyans.

THE CYCLOPS' RIVIERA
ACI TREZZA - ACI CASTELLO - CAPO MULINI

(Top): Panorama of Aci Trezza, the mythical scene of the Homeric legend of Ulysses. The rocks rising from the sea not far from the shore are the "Scogli dei Ciclopi" (Rocks of the Cyclops) which Polyphemus, blinded by Ulysses, hurled at the fleeing hero.

Aci Trezza is also famous as the scene of the famous novel "I Malavoglia" (English title: The House by the Medlar Tree) by **Giovanni Verga** (Catania 1840-1922), the great theorist of Italian literary Verism, a style connected with European Positivism and French Naturalism of which he was a major exponent in Sicily together with **Luigi Capuana** (Mineo 1839 - Catania 1915) and **Federico De Roberto** (Napoli 1861 - Catania 1927).

Bottom, right: **Aci Castello**, with the castle built in lava stone blocks on the top of a basaltic prysmatic lava crag. The Norman Castle was the property of Roger of Lauria who built it in 1076. Bottom, left: The rocky cliff of **Capo Mulini** reveals the natural beauty of this stretch of coast, with sharp contours and sheltered coves which are now renowned and busy bathing resorts.

TAORMINA

Tauromenion was founded by a group of survivors from Naxos, destroyed by Dionysius the Elder, tyrant of Syracuse, in 404 BC. Andromachus, father of the historian Timaeus, transferred the survivors on the slopes of Monte Tauro and founded the city in 358 BC. The foundation of the new Greek colony in the eastern part of the island caused the Sicel populations, who had already been compelled by the arrival of the first colonists to leave the coast and settle on the nearby Peloritani mountains, to move further inland. Tauromenion was never completely indepedent. It was often destroyed by the Greeks and the Carthaginians; during one of these attacks, the Greek historian Timaeus was exiled by the Syracusan tyrant Agathocles. At the beginning of the First Punic War the town allied with the Romans, who occupied it after the death of Hieron II making it a "civitas foederata". During the Roman age it witnessed important historical events, such as the slaves' revolt in 132 BC; it was pillaged by Verres, and turned into a colony by Octavian in 34 BC. In Byzantine times it was one of the key strongholds against the threatening Arabs; in 902 AD, a large part of its population was killed by the Arabs led by the cruel Ibrahim who, in front of the few survivors, pulled Bishop Procopius' heart out of his chest, eating it. Tauromenion enjoyed a short period of peace when the Christians rebuilt it in 913. In 962 the town, again under Muslim rule, was named "Almoezia" from the name of the conqueror, Al-Muizz. In 1079 Roger of Hauteville conquered it after a five-month siege. The Normans rebuilt and embellished Taormina, which became an important economic and commercial centre. In 1282, during the Vespers uprising, it remained loyal to Spain, siding with the Aragonese.

*Top: The side of the **Badia Vecchia** (Old Abbey) or **Badiazza**, a Norman building restored in the 14C with decorative motifs of the time.*
*Opposite page: The **Cathedral of San Nicola**, built in the 13C on the site of a pre-existing religious building, with the fountain dating from 1635. Restructured in the 15C and 16C, it still has the original portals and small rose window.*

In 1410 Palazzo Corvaia became the seat of the Sicilian Parliament which met in Taormina to elect Frederick, Count de Luna, as King of Sicily.

In 1675, during the Messina uprising, the town remained loyal to Spain and was occupied by the French soldiers of Louis XIV. During the Risorgimento, Filangeri became Duke of Taormina following the Bourbon recovery of 1848. The town showed its nationalist spirit in 1860, when Garibaldi's troops used it as a garrison.

As early as the 18C, having lost its former commercial role in that the new Messina-Catania road axis excluded the passage of goods and travellers from the town, Taormina became an elite tourist resort thanks to the foreign visitors who spread its historical and environmental image abroad. The town expanded beyond the boundary walls enclosing the Graeco-Roman old town centre, starting a process of tourist development which was to make it one of the most renowned tourist resorts in the world.

The old town centre includes monuments from every epoch: from the early Greek settlement and the Roman age, to the remains of Byzantine and medieval constructions, up to the 18C, Baroque and Catalan buildings.

CATHEDRAL OF SAN NICOLO'

The exterior of the basilica echoes the square architectural austerity of Norman cathedrals. The façade has a richly ornate portal with relief decorations framed by fine fluted columns, and a small 16C eight-mullioned rose window with a cross tracery in the middle.

On the left side is a late-15C portal with fine floreal decorations in the piers and ogee arch; in the centre of the architrave is Christ blessing flanked by St Peter and St Paul. On the right side there is a third portal dating from the first half of the 16C, with an ogival lunette and architrave. The interior is basilican in plan, with a nave and two aisles divided by six columns. The sacristy houses a rich collection of sacred gold items from various ages. Over the altars are paintings by **Antonino Giuffrè** (1463); a polyptych by **Antonello de Saliba** (1504); an alabaster statue of Virgin and Child (Gagini school, early 16C), and other valuable paintings and sculptures.

*On the following pages: A night view of the **Cathedral of San Nicola**, standing in the middle of the square flanked by the urban road with the remains of older buildings and 15C architectural vestiges.*
*Piazza IX Aprile and the **Church of Sant'Agostino.***

NAXOS

Two views of the remains of Naxos, the first Greek colony in Sicily, founded in 734 BC by the Chalcidians from Euboea led by the oecist Thucles. Archaeological investigation has found traces of earlier settlements, datable from the Neolithic (Stentinello culture) and the Bronze Age (Thapsos culture). As early as the archaic age, the city became culturally important as the seat of an altar dedicated to Apollo Archegetes (Founder), the protector of the Greek colonists in Sicily, built immediately after its foundation. During the following years, Naxos founded Leontinoi in 729 BC and Katane in 728 BC. Not far from the city, on a site not yet identified by archaeological research, the inhabitants of Naxos presumably founded the city of Callipolis. In 495 BC Hippocrates of Gela occupied and partly destroyed the city to oppose the Chalcidian expansionist policy. After recovering from this first Doric invasion, Naxos fell under the dominion of the Syracusan Hieron, brother and successor of Gelon, who deported its population to Leontinoi. In 425 BC it sided with Athens against Syracuse and, after the Athenian defeat in 414 BC, it suffered Dionysius the Elder's violent revenge in 403 BC, which caused its obliteration.

THE GRAECO-ROMAN THEATRE

The second most important and largest theatre in Sicily, surpassed only by the Greek theatre in Syracuse, it was started by Greek colonists in the 3C BC, during Hieron II's tyranny. In Roman Imperial times the building was altered and enlarged: the boundary walls were raised and the cavea widened, while the orchestra was left unchanged. The present aspect probably dates from the 2C BC, when it was almost completely restructured by the Romans who used it for gladiatorial fights. It has a maximum diameter of 109 m (35 m in the orchestra) and could seat 5,400 people.

The cavea, which exploits the morphology of the land, was divided into nine wedges, with masonry access steps; at the top, towards the exterior, there was a portico with large pillars, part of which has been restored and is visible today. The back walls of the stage are still extant, with niches and columns arbitrarily raised during restoration work carried out in 1860. The front had two orders of columns and the stage was flanked by the "parascenia", rooms used by the actors and for scenic fittings. In Roman times the theatre was only used for gladiato-rial and "venationes" shows. The orchestra was turned into an arena surrounded by a high podium which served as a protection for spectators during such dangerous performances, and by a service ambulatory with a vault supporting the lower steps. In the middle of the orchestra-arena were some large basins. The theatre still has excellent acoustics and, from the top of the steps, offers a magnificent view sweeping from the peak of Mount Etna, covered with snow for most of the wintertime, to the peninsula of Schisò, the site of ancient Naxos (the first Greek colony in Sicily), which seems to stretch out into the blue and pacific waters of the Ionian Sea, as far as the high peaks of Aspromonte, in Calabria, to the north.

Below: A detail of the stage, with a view of the imposing mass of Mount Etna. The brick scenic wall was preceded by a row of nine granite columns crowned by Corinthian capitals, which had both a decorative and bearing function, in that they supported the higher parts of the stage. The niches in the wall contained marble statues. On the sides, the remains of the "parascenia", square rooms used by the actors and for scenic fittings. The actors entered the stage through side openings. A further row of sixteen columns closer to the orchestra framed the decorative front of the stage.

Two spectacular 360° views of the **Graeco-Roman Theatre** and of the **belvedere gardens** in Taormina.

TAORMINA'S COASTLINE

The coast stretching from the long sandy shore of Letojanni to Capo Taormina is characterized by a succession of rocky promontories, enchanting bays, tiny golden beaches, marine grottoes and slender "faraglioni" (rocks) rising from the sea. On the mythical Ionian Sea, a beautiful natural scenery unfolds: **Baia delle Sirene** (Sirens' Bay), the cliffs of Capo Sant'Andrea dropping sheer into the sea, the charming gulf of **Isola Bella**, the rocky spur of Capo Taormina with the jagged **"faraglioni"** rising from the sea and the luminescent **Grotta Azzurra** (Blue Grotto). On the surrounding hills, covered with a lush vegetation and ever-green gardens, are the refined hotel facilities which have made Taormina famous all over the world. The town is also endowed with a mild winter climate and it thus may happen to see North-European tourists bathing in the **tepid waters of Mazzarò** in January, when Mount Etna is covered with snow and the early blossoming of almond-trees embellishes the gardens. For the Greeks, Sicily was a "gift of the Gods", a sort of promised land in view of its fertility, climate and unique natural beauties. Today the same good reasons, together with a historical and artistic heritage unequalled in Europe for the variety of epochs and cultures it embodies,

make Sicily worth visiting. Taormina is the shining example of these gifts which have come down to us through millennia of human history and evolution. The 18C travellers, who first disclosed the picturesque images of Taormina abroad in their paintings or early daguerrotypes, were the forerunners of an elite "tourist" inflow of European aristocrats and transoceanic visitors.

Since then Taormina has developed its tourist industry so as to become the main resort in Sicily thanks to its invaluable historical and natural heritage.

Above: The picturesque cove of **Lido Mazzarò**, *with the renowned bathing facilities and hotels in a refined and exclusive environment. Following pages: The charming* **Isola Bella** *(once a hermitic retreat), in a shining spring dawn.*

By turns a pitchy cloud she rolls on high;
By turns hot embers from her entrails fly,
And flakes of mountain flames, that lick the sky.
Oft from her bowels massy rocks are thrown,
And, shiver'd by the force, come piecemeal down.
Oft liquid lakes of burning sulphur flow,
Fed from the fiery springs that boil below.
(VIRGIL: Aeneid, III, 147, transl. by
J. Dryden, The Harvard Classics)

ETNA

Etna is the highest volcano in Europe and one of the most active in the world. Its majestic and imposing mass, about 3,300 m high, rises from the valley enclosed by the Alcantara and Simeto rivers in the Catania plain, overlooking the Ionian Sea, in the mythological scenery of the **Cyclops' Riviera**, and covering an area of 1,600 sq km. Its landscape has stirred the imagination of the ancients and inspired their myths as well as the works of great authors of all times.

The Greeks regarded it as the forge of **Hephaestus**, identified with the Roman god Vulcan, and as the house of the most tremendous of the Giants, **Enceladus**, son of Uranus and Gaea, who promoted the war of the Giants against Zeus and was thrown by the Lord of Olympus into the heart of the volcano, whence he still hurls fire at the sky. This mythological episode is taken from the **"Gigantomachy"**, the war of the Giants against the Olympian gods, of chaos against divine order.

ETNA NORD - The most interesting natural, historical and artistic itinerary, 135 km long, starts out from Catania passing through all the small towns situated on the slopes of the mountain, following a ring-like route which leads back to the city. From the northern suburbs of Catania, the coast road leads to the picturesque centres of Aci Castello (with the Norman Castle built in 1076), Aci Trezza (famous as the scene of the legendary adventures of *Ulysses* and of Verga's novel "I Malavoglia"), and Acireale (the Roman *"Akis"* sung by Ovid and Virgil, with the magnificent 17C monuments and the famous *"Santa Venera" Spa*, whose therapeutic waters were used by the Greeks and Romans).

The route goes on to Giarre and Riposto, then to Fiumefreddo di Sicilia, the ancient *"Flumen frigidum"*, where the road starts climbing up the lower slopes of Mount Etna, passing through Calatabiano and Linguaglossa, a holiday and winter sports resort. After a visit to the *"Alcantara Gorge"*, the route leads to Randazzo, 765 m above sea level, a town almost entirely built of lava stone, rich with Norman monuments. Leaving Randazzo, with a view of the majestic Etna, the road leads to the northern ski slopes of Piano Provenzano, at an altitude of 1,800 m above sea level.

Below: The telpher square (alt. 1,910 m), with the southern ski slopes. Right: Two views of the northern slope, with the ski lift facilities reaching an altitude of 2,350 m above sea level, beneath the peak of Monte Nero.

Photos: Some picturesque views of the Alcantara Gorge, attracting numerous tourist groups during a large part of the year.

GOLA DELL'ALCANTARA - The gorge was formed by the lava erupted in ancient times by the Moio crater and carved by the waters of the Alcantara river, which reaches the coast on the site where Naxos, the first Greek colony in Sicily, was founded. A visit to the picturesque green scenery, washed by the blue waters of the river, is a must. The river-bed can be reached on foot or by means of a comfortable lift which takes down to the entrance of the deep gorge, enclosed for more than twenty metres within two high lava walls which the elements have decorated with fantastic engravings and bizarre cavities producing a highly scenic effect.

The present name of the gorge, anciently called ***"Onobala"***, derives from the Arabic word ***"Al Cantara"***, i.e. the bridge across the river on the Roman consular road leading from Messina to Catania. The Alcantara river is very picturesque throughout its course, with short rapids alternating with placid, crystalline small lakes and, along the banks, a lush vegetation of rhododendrons, oleanders and tenacious brooms amid bright green crops.

MESSINA

The great Greek historian Thucydides thus reports on the foundation of Zancle (Messina):

"Zancle was originally founded by pirates from Cuma, the Chalcidian town in the country of the Opicans; afterwards, however, large numbers came from Chalcis and the rest of Euboea, and helped to people the place, the founders being Perieres and Crataemenes from Cuma and Chalcis respectively. It first had the name Zancle given it by the Sicels, because the place is shaped like a sickle, which the Sicels call "zanclon"; but upon the original settlers being afterwards expelled by some Samians and other Ionians who landed in Sicily flying from Medes, and the Samians in their turn not long afterwards by Anaxilas, tyrant of Rhegium, the town was by him colonized with a mixed population, and its name changed to Messina, after his old country" (transl. by R. Crawley, Encycl. Britannica Inc.). As reported by Strabo in his treatise of Italic geography: "Messene was founded by the Messenians of the Peloponnesus, who named it after themselves, changing its name; for formerly it was called Zancle, on account of the crookedness of the coast (anything crooked was called "Zanclion"), having been founded formerly by the Naxians, who lived near Catania. But the Mamertini, a tribe of the Campani, joined the colony later on" (transl. by H.L. Jones, Harvard University Press). The Romans used Messina as a base of operation for their Sicilian war against the Carthaginians; afterwards Sextus Pompey, when at war with Caesar Augustus, kept his fleet together there, and when ejected from the island also made his escape thence.

As in ancient times, Messina is a key city on the road network linking Sicily to the mainland, through the ferry service provided by both the Italian Railways and private companies. Bottom: The railway and maritime station of the Italian Railways, handling an intensive passenger and commercial traffic.

Top: The stele erected in 1934 on the ancient fort of San Salvatore, surmounted by a statue of the "Madonna of the Letter", with an inscription reading "Vos et ipsam civitatem benedicimus" taken from the letter that, according to tradition, the Virgin sent to the Messinese in 42 AD.

Above: The lake of Ganzirri, with mussel farms. High on the left, the two pylons of the power line linking Sicily to the mainland at the narrowest point of the Strait of Messina. In the foreground, the wide beaches of Punta Faro on the Tyrrhenian Sea, frequented by both residents and tourists.

Boats equipped for the fishing of swordfish in the surrounding waters sail off from the fishing village.
Below: Messina City Hall, built in 1924 to a neoclassical design by Antonio Zanca.

Cicero, who visited Messina while preparing his case against Verres for plunderage in various Sicilian cities, defined it "Civitas Maxima et locupletissima". The city allied with Syracuse against Carthage, was destroyed by the Carthaginians in 396 BC and later rebuilt by Dionysius of Syracuse. At the beginning of the First Punic War it was a Roman military base. The most prosperous period thus began for the city, on account of its strategic position on the road network linking Sicily to the Tyrrhenian and Ionian coasts on the mainland. Under Augustus, it was raised to the privileged status of "oppidum civium romanorum", a city administered through its own statutes. After the fall of the Western Roman Empire in 476 AD, Vandal and Goth invasions opened a dark period for the city, ending with the arrival of the Byzantines. The activities of the port were revived and the city recovered its original role as a key port of call in the trade relations between the Tyrrhenian and Ionian seas and the East. Thanks to its powerful walls, it offered a fierce resistance to the Muslim invasion of the island; it fell in 843, but part of the inhabitants fled to Rometta, where they organized a strong resistance which lasted for more than a century. The Normans, urged by the population to intervene against the Muslims, occupied Messina in 1061, and a period of economic and urban development began for the city. The Royal Palace, the Cathedral and the arsenal were built, and the city layout was reorganized; the building fever attracted people from Amalfi, Pisa, Genoa, Florence, Greece and Armenia, testifying to the splendid moment enjoyed by the city under the Norman and Swabian dynasties. Magnificent monuments were built: the churches of Santa Maria della Valle and the Annunziata dei Catalani (during Frederick II's Swabian rule); the San Salvatore cenobium, built by Count Roger in 1122-32 on the strip of land near the fort of Sant'Anna; the churches of Santa Maria degli Alemanni, the only example of Gothic architecture in Sicily, built by the Order of the Teutonic Knights in the 13C and restored by the city authorities in the post-war period, after centuries of neglect. At the end of the Norman-Swabian dy-

*The **Church of the Santissima Annunziata dei Catalani**, erected in the Norman period (second half of the 12C). In the surroundings was the six-towered castle built by Roger II, no more extant but celebrated in the bas-relief on the pedestal supporting the statue of Don John of Austria, victorious at Lepanto, placed in front of the church.*
In the photo, the original apse and external transept which, together with the cylindrical cupola, were left unaltered by the 13C remodellings, when the body of the church was shortened and the façade rebuilt. The interior is divided into a nave and two aisles by six monolithic columns bearing round arches.

nasty, the "evil Angevin rule", as Dante defined it, succeeded. The anti-Angevin uprisings in Palermo and the subsequent war of the "Sicilian Vespers" caused severe sufferings to Messina which, being a fortified city, was besieged by Charles of Anjou. The population, led by Alaimo, fought strenuously against the French troops; the figures of two heroines emerged, Dina and Clarenza, now celebrated on the Cathedral bell tower in two statues, ringing the bells of the city revolt. In 1535, Messina triumphally welcomed the Spanish Charles V, son of Joanna the Mad, King and Emperor of Sicily. Once again, thus, Sicily was ruled by a foreign power whose interests were in permanent conflict with those of the population, often harried and burdened with excessively high taxes. Messina revolted in 1674; it was besieged by the Spanish and suffered a violent repression which caused severe damage and depopulation. Those were dark centuries for the noble city of the Strait, as the impudent impositions by the foreign dominators were accompanied by a series of natural disasters. In 1743 an epidemic of plague killed more than 40,000 people; an earthquake in 1783 caused further death and destruction. Still oppressed by foreign rule under the Bourbons, Messina was torn by a series of rebellions and riots until 28 July 1860, when it was freed by Garibaldi's troops and became part of the Kingdom of Italy. In 1908 another earthquake, probably the most severe natural disaster ever suffered by the city, killed 60,000 people. Thanks to its industrious population, Messina was once again rebuilt with a view to guaranteeing the aseismic qualities of the new layout and buildings.

MESSINA CATHEDRAL (Duomo)

The most prestigious Norman monument in the city, it was started by Roger II in the early 12C; it was consecrated in 1187 in the presence of Henry IV of Swabia and dedicated to Santa Maria. The history of the church is marked by a series of disastrous events. As early as 1254, a fire destroyed the painted beams of the ceiling. In 1693 a succession of earthquakes began which also destroyed other Sicilian cities and towns. In 1783 another terrible earthquake destroyed the walls of the transept and the campanile. The 1908 earthquake gave the final blow, and the church was completely destroyed. Of the façade, only the left corner with the portal was spared; the side walls and right apse collapsed, and the other two were damaged. In 1919 the architect Francesco Valenti was entrusted with the reconstruction on the basis of the original Norman structure and the church was reopened on 13 August 1929.

In 1943 indiscriminate bombing by the Allies, who had occupied Sicily, caused death and destruction throughout the city: 94% of the buildings were damaged or razed to the ground, and the Cathedral was further damaged by a fire. Many works of art were destroyed, including the painting of the "Madonna of the Letter" (Byzantine school); the sarcophagi of Conrad IV of Hohenstaufen, King of Sicily from 1250 to 1254, and Alfonso of Aragon "The Magnanimus", King of Sicily from 1416 to 1458; the mosaic decorations; the bronze baldachin and other unvaluable masterpieces such as the frescoes by G.B. Quagliata, the wooden choir and the marble inlaid floor. In the post-war period the original Norman structures were reconstructed and the destroyed decorations restored. The basilican-plan interior is divided into a nave and two aisles by two lines of 26 monolithic columns, with three apses and a transept covered, in the central nave, by trusses decorated with figures of Saints, Angels, Apostles and Evangelists. The main portal was built by Pietro di Bonitate and G.B. Mazzolo between the end of the 14C and 1534. It has at both sides lions supporting twisted columns and five orders of small statues. In the ogee arch is a "Madonna enthroned with Child", sculptured by G.B. Mazzolo in 1534 and, in the carved spire on the top, "Christ crowning the Virgin" with exultant angels on the three points, sculptured by Pietro Bonitate in 1464-77.

The slender campanile, 60 m high, stands to the left of the Cathedral. It was designed by Francesco Valenti and inaugurated on 13 August 1933. The mechanical clock, with automatic figures and dials with the perpetual calendar and the moon phases, was built by Ungerer, a Strasbourg-based firm, and is regarded as the biggest in the world. On the southern side, facing the Cathedral, are the dials with the calendar and planetary system. On the western side are automatic sculptured figures referring to the religious and historical life of the city. Every day, as noon strikes, all the figures on the west side start to move, creating the spectacle designed by their maker.

THE CAMPANILE OF MESSINA CATHEDRAL

At noon, all the animated figures of the campanile start moving in succession, creating allegorical representations of episodes from the historical and religious life of the city, accompanied by a sacred music background.

The roaring lion carrying the flag starts the movements of the various groups; it is a symbol of the indomitable will of the Messinese thoughout their long history.

The double-light window with the hour-bell (1590) and the quarter-bell (1679). In the centre, a golden cock crowing and, to the sides, the statues of **Dina** and **Clarenza**, the two heroines of the popular insurrection against Charles of Anjou's troops in August 1282, striking the hours.

In this scene, the letter from the Virgin is delivered by an angel to the four bowing Messinese ambassadors, preceded by St Paul.

The tableau with the four scenes from the Gospel: the **Holy Crib**, **Epiphany**, **Resurrection** and **Pentecost**, appearing in succession to represent the four main religious feasts.

The tableau with the **Sanctuary of Montalto**, sacred to the Vespers, and the dove flying and pointing to the plan of the building with its right wing.

The representation of the **four human ages**, one every fifteen minutes: childhood, youth, adulthood and old age; in the end, death appears, holding the scythe.

The scene of the two-wheeled charriot pulled by a deer, indicating the day of the week as it goes by.

THE SOUTHERN SIDE OF THE CAMPANILE

The Globe showing the moon phases.

The planetary system dial, with a 5-m diameter and a 35-wheel mechanism.

The calendar dial, 3.5 m in diameter, with an inscription showing the date of construction of the clock.

MILAZZO

Evidence of an early Neolithic settlement dating from c 4000 BC has been found in the territory of Milazzo. Between the 9C and 8C BC the site was inhabited by the Sicels, until the foundation of the Greek city of **Mylai** in 649 BC on the lower slopes of the narrow peninsula which characterizes the coastal area. Excavations carried out on the site of the necropolis have brought to light a proto-Villanovan cremation burial system referrable to the 10C-8C BC, with bowl-covered urns surrounded by stones. Tomb furnishings dating from the period following the foundation of the Greek city (8C-7C BC) and including proto-Corinthian, Ionic and Cycladian pottery have also been found in the necropolis. During the Punic Wars, in 260 BC, the battle between Carthaginians and Romans, won by Consul Caius Duilius, was fought in the waters off Milazzo. In Norman times, the city was fortified and in the 13C Frederick II of Swabia erected the powerful castle which the Spanish of Ferdinand of Aragon surrounded with walls in the 16C. In July 1860, Milazzo was the scene of Garibaldi's victory over the Bourbons.

From the lighthouse at Capo Milazzo there is a splendid view of the Aeolian islands, the Calabrian coast and the Nebrodi and Peloritani mountains. A flight of steps near the lighthouse leads up to the rock sanctuary where St Anthony of Padua took refuge while voyaging from Africa to Lisbon.

*Top: Panorama of **Milazzo**, highlighting the various stages of urbanisation. The citadel surrounded by the 16C walls, the Borgo with the **"Spanish quarters"** and the low-lying modern town developing around the port. Left: The slender, intensively cultivated peninsula ending at Capo Milazzo, fringed with picturesque coves and small beaches where villas surrounded by luxuriant gardens have been built.*

AEOLIAN OR LIPARI ISLANDS

The Aeolian Islands, the **"seven sisters"**, all share the same Quaternary volcanic origin and were formed as a result of the millenary accumulation of eruptive material and raising of the sea floor. Only two volcanoes of the vast original system are still active today. **Vulcano**, which last erupted in 1888-90, now limits its activity to the emission of hot sulphurous gases. **Stromboli** still has a cyclic eruptive activity, accompanied by explosions of scoriae, lava and vapours which are thrown high into the sky precipitating along paths known as "sciare di fuoco", like torrents of fire, into the sea.

Archaeological investigation has continued ever since 1946 thanks to the Soprintendenza ai Beni Culturali (Cultural Heritage Authority) of Eastern Sicily. Excavations have suggested that the settlements in Lipari, from the 4th millennium BC onwards, might be the result of migratory flows from the Sicilian coasts, on account of the decorated pottery in the style peculiar to the so-called Stentinello culture found on the mountainous spurs of Lipari. After various periods (classified as Milazzese, Ausonius I and II, from 1400 to the 7C BC), Greek civilisation began in 580 BC, when the Cnidians, back from Pentathlus' unsuccessful expedition, landed at Lipari and founded their colony (Diodorus Siculus).

Until the Roman conquest, Lipari followed the fortunes of Sicily in the wider context of the secular struggles among Greeks, Carthaginians and Romans to gain control of the island. In 836 AD the Arabs destroyed Lipari and it was only under Roger, Norman Count of Sicily from 1083, that the island and the Archipelago revived, also thanks to an active group of Benedictine monks who founded a monastery on the ancient Acropolis by Norman decree.

Photos: A stretch of the southern coast at **Punta Crapazza**, *Lipari. Below: Panorama of the town with its natural stronghold, the site of the Neolithic, Graeco-Roman, Norman medieval and 18C settlements.*

Above: The magnificent view from the edge of the **Gran Cratere della Fossa**, one of the craters on the island of Vulcano. In the foreground, the "fumaroles" of the Gran Cratere, and the small peninsula of **"Vulcanello"**, with the secondary volcano risen from the sea in 183 BC, as reported by Pliny. The eruptive activity ceased in the 1880s. Volcanic activities are now limited to the emission of gas along the edge of the crater and to the boiling sea-water phenomenon and sulphurous vapours which can be seen along the water line facing Porto di Levante, where excellent therapeutic mud baths can be taken. In the background, the mountainous profile of Lipari, the chief town of the Archipelago. Of extreme interest is a visit to the Castle housing the **Aeolian Archaeological Museum** (Museo Archeologico Eoliano), with archaeological material from

long excavation campaigns displayed in a strictly chronological order from the prehistoric to medieval ages, a testimony to the plurimillenary history of the Archipelago.

This includes seven islands: Lipari, Vulcano, Salina, Panarea, Filicudi, Alicudi and Stromboli *(see photo above)* and the emerging uninhabited islets of Strombolicchio, 1500 m far from Stromboli, and Basiluzzo, near Panarea. Stromboli is itself a volcano, which has been active for more than two thousand years, and the youngest island of the Archipelago. Its name derives from the Greek word "Strongyle", meaning "round", from the rounded top of the volcano. The island has been inhabited since the Upper Neolithic, some 3000 years ago, as shown by archaeological evidence of settlements dating from that period. Other archaeological finds have been related to the Piano Conte cultural "facies" (2500 BC); an early Bronze Age village has also been discovered, related to the Capo Graziano "facies" and datable from 1500 BC. Tombs dating from the 4C BC and the Roman age have been brought to light at contrada Ficogrande.

TINDARI

Founded in 396 BC by Dionysius the Elder, it was one of the latest Greek colonies in Sicily. It rises on a stretch of level ground on the top of the Capo Tindari promontory, on a picturesque site overlooking the sea. The Greek **Tyndaris** was a prosperous centre and witnessed a monumental urban development, particularly in Roman times. A loyal Roman ally against Carthage during the Punic Wars, it was a privileged city during the Imperial Age, as confirmed by both historical sources and archaeological research. It was built to a regular plan, with wide parallel streets (decumani) crossed by a series of perpendicular narrow lanes (cardines) forming the "insulae", blocks of private houses flanked by shops and tabernae with rooms arranged around a peristyle. According to Pliny, a considerable part of the city collapsed into the sea in the 1C AD owing to a landslide. In the early centuries of Christianity and under the Byzantines it was raised to a diocese, but it was completely destroyed during the Arab conquest. On the high-

est point of Capo Tindari, probably on the site of the ancient Acropolis, is the sanctuary of the **"Madonna di Tindari"** with the Byzantine wooden statue of the **"Black Madonna"**, attracting the devotion of many worshippers and traditionally believed to be of Oriental origin. The sanctuary was built in 1549 on the site of a pre-existing one, after the town was destroyed and sacked by the North-African pirate Ariadeno Barbarossa. In the photos on the left, from top to bottom: The extant columns of a Roman villa dating from the second half of the 1C AD. The cavea of the Greek theatre, dating from the 3C-2C BC. The so-called Basilica or gymnasium, the late-Imperial public meeting-place. In the plate, a picturesque view of the Sanctuary of the Black Madonna, with the small Vergolo, Verde and Marinello lagoons, enclosed by gravel banks constantly altered in contour and width by the action of the sea.

CONTENTS

Printed by : Officine Grafiche Riunite - Palermo
April 2004